Freda Marnie Nicholls began her w
to the editor of a dirt bike magazine, compla...
fact that she was being left to bring up three little children
while her husband was off riding his bike in his spare time.
This tongue-in-cheek letter led to a monthly column and
gave her the courage to pursue her dream of writing around
farming, work and family activities.

Freda lives and works on her husband's family farm in
beautiful southern New South Wales and has worked for
various national magazines and newspapers, even working
as editor for one regional paper for a short time, before
realising it was more fun helping on the farm and writing
on a freelance basis.

Freda has written articles for *The Land*, *Canberra
Times* and regional papers, numerous horse and lifestyle
magazines, including various publications of RM Williams
Outback Publishing, writing mostly about rural people and
their lives.

Her first book, *Love, Sweat & Tears*, was published in
2013.

BACK OF
BEYOND

Freda Marnie Nicholls

ALLEN&UNWIN

SYDNEY•MELBOURNE•AUCKLAND•LONDON

Dedicated to the hard-working
men and women of Australia

First published in 2014

Allen & Unwin
Sydney, Melbourne, Auckland, London

83 Alexander Street
Crows Nest NSW 2065
Australia
Phone: (61 2) 8425 0100
Fax: (61 2) 9906 2218
Email: info@allenandunwin.com
Web: www.allenandunwin.com

Cataloguing-in-Publication details are available
from the National Library of Australia
www.trove.nla.gov.au

ISBN 978 1 74331 716 7

Set in 12/18 pt Sabon by Post Pre-press Group, Australia
Printed and bound in Australia by Griffin Press

10 9 8 7 6 5 4 3 2 1

The paper in this book is FSC® certified.
FSC® promotes environmentally responsible,
socially beneficial and economically viable
management of the world's forests.

Contents

Chapter 1

Poddy dodgers' paradise

MY FIRST MEMORIES are of dry whirly winds. Winds straight off the Simpson Desert; hot winds that would stir the dirt into every nook and cranny, into your eyes, your ears, and through the open fire, mixing gidgee ash into Mum's damper.

My Dad, Arthur, successfully drew a 'selection' in 1924, two years before I was born. He named it Red Knob after a small red rise on the boundary of the 31,000 acres (12,500 hectares) of sparse scrubby plains that were to be our home. It was one of eight selections drawn off the edge of Warbreccan Station, 150 mile (240 kilometres) west of Longreach in Central West Queensland.

When the first white people went out into that country, they'd say, 'My place runs between that mountain and that river.' And that was it. There were certainly no surveyors, and the more remote places, like Warbreccan on the channel country in the Diamantina, were over a million acres. Those big blocks were leased from the government, but later on the government took small portions off the edge of them and balloted them off. It encouraged people out into the bush, who then paid a lease fee to the government. Selections were by ballot, almost a lucky dip. There were a lot of selections balloted off after both the First and Second World Wars for returned soldiers, with a few ballots in the surrounding years for whoever wanted to have a go at living on the land.

When you drew a selection you had to go out and live on the block within a certain amount of time in order to claim it. But if the country wasn't much good or there wasn't good water it was hard to make a living out there; if they couldn't make a go of it, some people left the blocks, which would then be 'resumed' back by the government and balloted off again.

Red Knob was a terrible drought-stricken place. It had loose, pale, ashy soil with little or no scrub, and most people thought it was too small to make an honest living on. They called it a 'poddy dodgers' paradise'. Poddy dodging is when unbranded calves or 'poddies' are mustered off big properties and branded by the 'dodger' or thief with their own brand. As far as I know, Dad wasn't involved with any poddy dodging—he always despised liars and thieves and was constantly checking his boundaries. In any case, he only ran sheep out there.

It was a depressing sort of place, split in two by a rickety old fence. It was a long way from anywhere and was light-carrying country, not able to carry many sheep through lack of water and feed. The six-foot dingo-proof fence on our western boundary was the last sheep fence out there; after that just the Diamantina and Georgina rivers, which only ran water during the wet season, lay between the Simpson Desert and us.

When you drew a selection, you had to improve the block, clear any timber and build dams, and a certain amount had to be spent on it. If the block was later resumed, you wouldn't usually be compensated for any improvements, like dams or houses. So it was generally expected that anything built was for your use only, nothing more. It was fairly basic living.

First thing Dad did when he got out to Red Knob was build a 30-by-20-foot (nine-by-six-metre) bough shed. It consisted of four rough posts made from the boughs of trees, with four open sides and a cane-grass roof, held down with wire to stop it blowing off. Cane grass looks a bit like miniature bamboo—it stands three to four foot (around a metre) high and grew mainly around the watercourses and swamps. It was plentiful and so a lot of early huts were thatched with cane grass. Dad then put a few coolabah leaves on top of it, to keep off the worst of the sun. It didn't keep out the rain, but then it didn't really rain much out there anyway. He also had a tent, but it was too hot to use in summer, so we put bullock hides on the ground at night and slept on them under the bough shed.

We all travelled there from Nyngan, in central New South Wales, when I was not quite two. Mum, Dad, my older brother Arthur, me, my new baby brother Godfrey, two thousand sheep, a couple of horses, Dad's working dogs, a Model T Ford utility and Dad's pride and joy, his 1926 Buick. The Buick was really something in those days—it was too good to use all the time, so it would just stay with us under the bough shed.

It was a pretty rough turn going out there with three young boys, but Dad wanted to make a go of it. He had first met my Mum Ada when she was working at the refreshment room at the Narromine railway station. Even though her people were from Narromine, a farming town west of Dubbo, Mum hadn't been on the land before, but it was par for the course in those times—she just followed her husband and did what needed to be done.

Mum cooked our food over an open fire in the corner of the shed, protected on two sides by six-foot lengths of corrugated iron. If we got a whirly wind come through off the desert we'd have pots and pans going everywhere, but not the cast-iron camp ovens, they were too heavy. Ash would fly everywhere, but you didn't worry about that. Good clean ash never hurt anybody—it just made the damper taste a bit funny, that's all.

Dad could write and add up money, but he had had very little formal education. His mum, my grandmother, had a small selection called Pangee at Bobadah, near Nyngan. Until he was fifteen, Dad lived there with his parents, his older brother and five sisters. The blocks were too small to really make a living on—they were called 'heartbreak blocks', with poor sandy country and full of native pine. Pangee was another selection that had originally been taken off a big property, Overflow Station, and it was in the middle of a bad drought when Dad left.

Dad had worked in a coal mine as a billy boiler at the age of eleven, but in 1911, when he was fifteen, he bought a pushbike and went out into the world. He made his way down to Sydney and then, for some unknown reason, decided to get on a boat and travel up to Cairns in Far North Queensland. He then cycled from Cairns out onto the Atherton Tablelands, looking for work, before he rode further out west to Hughenden on the Flinders River, and eventually got a job driving a horse team. He heard they were putting down a bore on Redcliffe Station, a place just out of Hughenden, and he worked there for a while. When that finished he rode down through Aramac and Barcaldine to Blackall in Central West Queensland and got a job laying the new railway line out to Yaraka from Blackall—tough hot work.

When he heard that the drought had broken back in Nyngan, he decided to head home. He cycled down through Charleville to Pangee. I don't know how long it took him, but it would have been a slow old trip on a pushbike on rough dirt roads.

Dad eventually got a block near his parents and siblings on a place he called Rosewood. But that trip into Queensland, seeing that country and working in it, must have made an impression, because when he saw the Warbreccan selection come up for ballot twelve years later, he didn't hesitate to apply.

We went from that small heartache block at Nyngan to the worst country out on the headwaters of the Diamantina. Red Knob was on Farrars Creek, which didn't always run water. There were no roads along Farrars Creek—you just made your way through properties, opening and closing gates as you went. The nearest neighbour was fifteen mile south-west of us and we had no means of communication. We rarely saw people, other than an occasional neighbour.

Dad fixed the fence dividing the place and fenced off a smaller 1000-acre horse paddock near the shed. Dividing the place into at least two main paddocks meant that when he shore our sheep he could separate them, putting the shorn sheep in one paddock and keeping the woolly sheep in the other. All the ewes, wethers (castrated rams) and lambs ran together, and the rams were kept in the horse paddock when they weren't out with the ewes. There were no big holding yards, so when we were shearing, Dad had to go and collect enough sheep for a day's shearing. It was almost a day's travel out on horseback to the back of the place before Dad even started mustering the sheep back in, so shearing was a long, drawn-out process.

The first shearing I remember seeing, when I was about two or three, was done in our bough shed. Dad and another chap, Hughie McKeller, who Dad paid to come out and help, used the bullock hides we slept on as a board to try and keep the wool out of the dirt. They used sharp hand shears that had a piece of leather at the base of the blades, where the blades joined the handles, to stop the jarring action when you opened and closed them. After about two hours of steel hitting steel, they'd have had bad wrists, so they put leather there to soften the movement. The shears made more of a swish sound than a click like in the song, but 'Swish Goes the Shears' doesn't really have the same ring to it.

I remember watching the razor-sharp blades slide the wool off onto the bullock hides. Dad and Hughie guided the blades along, turning the sheep around with practised skill to remove the fleece in one go. The smell of a freshly shorn fleece, the feel of its oily softness and the sight of its creamy white length topped with a thin dark outer layer of dust and dirt—at that age I had no idea how important wool would be throughout my life.

Chapter 2

Life on the edge of the big stations

BACK IN 1900, the original Warbreccan Station was said to have employed over a hundred people and to have had its own store, village and school. It was still over one million acres when we went out there, and managed to employ thirty people, including station hands, fencers and dingo trappers. All of that country is infested with dingoes; Warbreccan used to have a couple of dingo trappers on all of the time and they only just kept the thick of them away. The dingoes used to look after the sheep, kill them if we weren't all on guard, and it was a constant battle when they made it through the dingo-proof fence, which would happen if say a post rotted or wire corroded or a hole was made by kangaroos and emus.

Mum was sometimes able to buy fresh vegies from one of the two Chinese gardeners who worked on the station. The idea was that the gardeners didn't get paid by the station but they could sell extra produce if there was an oversupply of something in season. There were a lot of travelling drovers, fencers or people passing through who'd pull into the big stations, go down and see the gardener, and anything the station didn't use the gardener could sell and name their price. So the gardeners used to be on quite a good wicket.

Fresh fruit and green vegies were pretty rare for us. We lived on mostly corned (salted) meat, potatoes, pumpkins, onions, flour, tea and sugar. Mum occasionally made her own bread if she had some yeast; otherwise we'd have dampers made out of flour and water. In the pudding line we used to eat a lot of rice, tapioca and sago. Mum would get supplies on her rare trips to Longreach, usually once or twice a year, or they would be delivered with the mail truck that came out once a week in the dry season. There was no refrigeration in the bough shed, and despite Mum's tin-lined storage boxes weevils got into everything, but you just had to sieve them out before using the flour or skim them off the top of the water when cooking the rice. They didn't really eat much.

Sunday was a real red-letter day—one day a week we'd have a tin of fruit, a highlight of our diet. Sometimes, also on a Sunday, Dad would take us out and we'd shoot a bustard or a wild turkey for some fresh meat all year round. After the wet season, in say March or April, lots of ducks would come in—wood ducks, teals and whistlers—and so we'd have a fair amount of duck meat that time of year. We only really shot birds for Christmas or Sunday dinner, though, just for a change from corned meat.

At Christmas we would usually go to the bigger Connemara or Vergemont stations, both about 60 mile away from us, or, in later years, they would come to us for a couple of days of socialising. We certainly never had lollies as kids, but we always had a rooster or bush turkey for Christmas lunch, sometimes ham, and the all-important plum pudding for dessert. Mum always put a thruppence in the pudding, and to find that—well, it was the best thing.

One Christmas at Vergemont, us kids decided to introduce the two Aboriginal stockmen working on the place to Christmas lunch. They both sat at a table outside and us kids took them out plate after plate of bush turkey and ham, which they kept eating. When it came to the plum pudding, they could no longer speak—they could only grunt and groan as they tried to fit that in as well. We couldn't believe they were able to eat it all, and they couldn't believe the never-ending food.

Aboriginal stockmen having Christmas lunch at Vergemont homestead.

Because of the lack of fresh fruit and vegetables we used to get barcoo rot, an outback version of scurvy, which is caused by a lack of vitamin C in the diet. Everyone had it, especially children, but Mum and Dad didn't know why. You'd get a little scratch and it would sort of burn, sting like slight sunburn, and it got bigger and bigger until it was about the size of a twenty-cent piece. It wasn't as painful as it looked—it would fill with pus underneath, and would then get a nasty-looking scab on it, which would eventually just fall off. But as soon as you went away somewhere and had a few oranges and vegetables, this barcoo rot would go.

The other one we used to get out there was sandy blight, or trachoma, like a lot of the Aboriginal kids at the time. It's a type of conjunctivitis, and it's extremely contagious and spread by the ordinary little bush flies that constantly surrounded us. It would start off as a bung eye and it felt just like you had sand in your eyes; it looked like a real shiner, like someone had stuffed an egg under your eyelids, and you wouldn't be able to see.

We got sandy blight mostly at the beginning of the year, after the rains and through the summer heat. At that time of year you just couldn't keep the flies off—there were clouds of them around you during the day. Then of course after the rivers had gone down there would be swarms of sand flies. When they were at their worst, you'd see them just like clouds, like moving smoke. The horses would walk a mile out into the rivers if they could, just to get away from them. We had the sand flies in daylight and mosquitoes at night, but real smoky fires kept the worst of the insects away. I think blight had something to do with deficiency too, but I just don't know. People who had an orange or lemon tree didn't seem to get it as much. I haven't seen either blight or barcoo rot for over fifty years.

Because we didn't have any vegies or fibre in our diet, sometimes we'd have a little bit of bowel trouble, and Mum would issue out a big spoonful of castor oil to each of us. Sometimes we'd start up a bit of a 'donnybrook'—a fight—and Mum'd reckon our bowels mustn't have been working, so as a punishment she'd give us a spoonful of castor oil, and of course we'd be so busy running to the toilet it would stop us fighting.

Bush remedies were important out in that isolated country—a doctor could be hundreds of miles away, and the Royal Flying Doctor Service didn't start up out there until the end of the 1930s. Before then we didn't have any proper medical kits—maybe a few bandages, scissors, sewing needles and sticking plaster. We usually had aspirin for pain relief, iodine to dab on sores and cuts, Epsom salt (magnesium sulfate) for aches and pains, and the dreaded castor oil. Mum would mix castor oil with something called iodoform and put it on our sores—it would keep the flies off as well as help the sores to heal, but it smelt pretty terrible.

We also had a bottle of friar's balsam, which is stronger than iodine and was used on cuts to stop infection, because there was no such thing as antibiotics then. Friar's used to burn like hell when you put it on a cut. Dad used it more than us—it burnt too much, so we were happy with the iodine. Mum also used to keep Eno's fruit salts as a pick-me-up, and to make you go as well. A dose of Eno's would certainly make something happen!

Eighteen months after Godfrey was born, Lachlan William arrived. Mum and Dad now had four boys under six years of age. Hygiene was a bit rough and ready because water was so scarce. We had a big round tub, two foot (60 centimetres) across the top, and everyone bathed in the same water. The cleanest of the kids, usually the baby, went in first, and the dirtiest went in last.

We used to have to cart the water from the only muddy waterhole on Farrars Creek on a horse-drawn dray with a 100-gallon (450-litre) tank on the back. We'd back it down to the edge, throw a four-gallon bucket down, bring it up full of water and throw the water into the tank. Once it was full we'd drive the mile or so back to the bough shed and syphon the water out of the dray tank into an open tank that stood three foot tall and five foot wide near the shed. Every scrap of water we used had to be carted, because even when it did rain we didn't have a tin roof for any water to run off. Some of the bigger stations had tin roofs and a few showers for their men, but the ordinary cockies went there with nothing and spent their life out there with nothing.

After carting the water, it would be all stirred up, so we'd throw a couple of handfuls of gidgee ash into the open tank to settle the mud. Gidgee burns very hot and for longer than some of the other native trees and produces a lot of fine white talc-like ash, which won't hurt you if you drink it. If you burn ironbark or gum, the ash is sort of brown and there will be quite a lot of charcoal, but with gidgee the whole lot of it burns and there is virtually no charcoal. A day after throwing the ash in the water, the mud settles and it becomes clear. About once a year we had to clean out the tank and remove the ash and mud that had settled on the bottom.

When we first started handfeeding our pet or poddy lambs or kangaroos, they would often get stomach aches because they weren't used to drinking cows' or goats' milk, we'd crush up charcoal into a fine powder and put it into the milk to stop the dysentery ('the scours', we used to call it). And it worked. We had poddies—orphaned animals—all the time. If it wasn't pigs or kangaroos, it would be lambs or puppies or something.

I must have been about seven when I caught a wild piglet one time as we were coming across the Thomson River on the way back from Longreach, and of course I made a pet of him. A pig is one of the best pets a boy could ever get, even better than a dog—they just love you for what you are. I think they think they are a kid or a dog themselves. 'Pig' would often follow us down to the waterhole if it was hot and have a swim with us, because there was no water around the house for him to wallow in. He grew big and fat, and I tried to ride him down to the dam a few times but he didn't like that much.

Our cane-grass hut had a big open fireplace at one end, and at night in the wintertime the pig would come in and lie in the ash for warmth. When Dad woke up early in the morning and went to stoke up the fire, the pig often wouldn't move, so Dad used to stoke up the fire beside him. Dad always swore he could smell bacon cooking before the pig would take off squealing.

Everyone out there had goats for meat and fresh milk, and we'd make pets out of the odd castrated billy that we were fattening. When we were a bit older, us kids made our own billy cart. It was just a wooden box base with a couple of wheels; we added two long shafts to go either side of the billy and hooked him into it, but he never wanted to go. I'd reach over and twitch his tail and he would take off, but then we were in trouble because we couldn't turn or stop him, so that was no good.

We had pet galahs and magpies too. And of course we always had dogs. You can't work sheep in those places without dogs. A good dog is worth three men. You'd get them for nothing as pups—somebody had a good dog and you'd ask them to keep a pup for you, and it would grow into a good dog and then somebody else would say, 'I'd like a pup out of him,' and that way the good working blood-lines continued.

Dad only had two or three dogs at one time. Generally, if you see somebody with a mob of dogs, most of them aren't worth much. Two really good dogs are all you need, three at the most. Once you've got one dog going, you can put a little six-week-old pup with a trained dog, often their mother, and they just watch and learn.

I've always said you should never have a sheepdog in town—they get bored. They are bred to work and they live to work, and they love it. Sometimes, in real hard country, they'll work until the pads of their feet wear off and you have to put little leather lace-up boots on them. They can be that sore-footed they can hardly walk, but they will still want to keep going. They won't even stop when they have a goathead seed or a bindi-eye sticking into their feet; if you don't get those out early on, they can get in a mess, poor buggers.

We always tied our young dogs up at night, or kept them in a run. The older ones you wouldn't worry about as much, but you wouldn't know what trouble the young ones'd get up to at night—they could wander off and get lost, or kill or maim a young sheep. You just let them out in the morning, and they can be off with you all day. Some people don't let them off every day—they leave them tied up if they're not working. I think that's terrible, but anyway, everyone has their own ideas.

The thing is with a good working dog, he's your work-mate. You don't have to supply him with a bed, he's happy to dig a bit of a hole, and he's happy to have something to eat at night and a crust or two while you're having lunch. I had a few favourite dogs over time, no money could have bought them from me—they were worth so much to me, even more than just a workmate. When I finished up, I wouldn't sell my last dog; instead I lent him to a bloke I trusted, permanently.

It was rare to use the vehicles on the place; most of the work was done with horses. The Model T Ford utility was first made in about 1910. Henry Ford made them in America and apparently he said, 'You can have any colour you like, as long as it's black.' It had a four-cylinder engine and was a great little bush car—it could get up to about 30 mile an hour, had great ground clearance, could go through mud in the wet season, go through anything. For grip in the mud, we'd wrap chains around the skinny tyres and through the spokes of the wheel, and plough on through.

To start the Model T you had to crank the engine with the big crank handle on the front. It didn't have a self-starter, or gears—just one low gear. It had a reverse pedal and a forward gear; to move forward, you put your foot on a pedal like a clutch, put it in gear, then it had a long hand-brake lever you pushed in to release, and away you went. There was no accelerator pedal, just a lever underneath the steering wheel, and you pushed that around to accelerate. The Model T would drive along so slowly that you'd never wear out the tyres.

The fuel came in these square four-gallon cans. They were packed in a wooden case, which fitted two cans of fuel snugly, so we'd buy petrol by the case. They were beautiful pine cases, and we made all sorts of things out of them—cupboards, tables and seats. Even the cans were used to make things; they could be turned into wash-up tins, or used for pot plants and buckets. It was the standard thing—everybody had square four-gallon buckets and pine-case furniture.

Fuel was about a shilling a gallon then, which is four and a half litres. It was so cheap by today's standards, but we still complained about the price. It took two cases of fuel in the Buick to make it from Red Knob to Longreach, the largest town in the region. We only went a couple of times a year. Sometimes we might go to Stonehenge for a sports day or horse races or something like that; it was our closest town—if you could call it a town—about 80 mile away to the east. It had a pub and a police station, four or five houses, but no store. A further 40 mile past that was Jundah, which had a store and was a bit bigger than Stonehenge. When you grew up with that, and then went into Longreach, dear oh dear, it was really something.

Chapter 3

The biggest town in the world

THERE IS A main road that follows the river from Longreach to Jundah and the locals called it the 'Down the River Road'. It was never really formed when we first went out there—it was just the quickest way to Longreach. A graded road and stock grids were eventually put in by the Longreach council in the late 1930s, as too many people were travelling through and leaving gates open. The 'road' was a few mile out from the channels, but it still went under water in a flood.

To get to Longreach in the Buick we had to cross the Vergemont Creek. Twenty-four creeks and rivers flow into the Vergemont, which then flows into the Thomson. Each creek produces a channel, and there were two main channels we had to cross to get to Longreach, Stonehenge or Jundah. The channels were eroded sections, running in the direction of the flow but particularly deep and wide. Unless there was a flood, there was never any water in them.

It would take us all day to get to Longreach. We'd take our swags, and for the first few years we camped on the outskirts of town at Gin Creek. (It's been renamed, because someone somewhere reckoned it was politically incorrect, but I don't know its name now—it'll always be Gin Creek to me.) The next day we'd be in our very best clothes, ready to go into town, but none of us had any boots—I don't think I had a pair of my own until I was about fourteen. Dad would go into town first thing in the morning and buy a dozen buns and four loaves of beautiful fresh white bread—real bread, not like Mum's damper with specks of ash through it. Mum and Dad would do the jobs and shopping they needed to do, and then our treat was a penny ice cream and the pictures. (I remember one year when we were even shouted a threepenny ice cream and we talked about it for weeks, because ice cream in those days was the ultimate treat. We just didn't have it—we had no refrigeration, let alone a freezer.)

Going to the movies before Christmas was a big deal; for weeks beforehand we'd be wondering what was on at the pictures. We always liked the Buck Rogers movies or something like that; cowboy movies were our favourites. The next day we'd have a full day travelling home, with memories of movie stars and exciting adventures, together with the delights of fresh hot bread and freezing-cold ice cream, to sustain us until the following year. Treats were few and far between, and those memories stayed with us all year.

I thought Longreach was the biggest town in the world; I didn't think anything could be bigger. There were a thousand people in the town and another eight hundred in the surrounding district, and to me it was huge. We'd usually make the annual trip just before Christmas—before the start of the wet season and before we were flooded in. You get the monsoons out there to the north and they generally come from December to March bringing the rains that eventually flowed into the Vergemont Creek and Thomson River, and then it dries off and you might not even get a sprinkle of rain for the rest of the year.

Floods were more or less annual out there; sometimes the river only came up in the two main channels of the Vergemont, but it was still difficult to cross. The only way to get to Longreach in flood time was to go down the river to Stonehenge, and then travel by road back up to Longreach. Every wet season we would usually get cut off. Even if it only rained for a week, nobody would be able to get anywhere for a month afterwards, as you'd get bogged.

We used to get mail once a week, except in the wet season. Jim Doyle delivered the mail, food and farm supplies in his big 1920 Hudson Dodge truck. He would come down 100 mile to Stonehenge from Longreach on his run and then make his way west. If the river was in flood, the mail would have to wait at Stonehenge the six weeks or more it took for the floodwaters to go down, unless we rowed across the six miles (ten kilometres) of swollen Thomson River to get it. Sometimes it took three months for the floodwaters to subside.

The headwaters of the Thomson River start up near Afton Downs, just a few mile south of Hughenden, on the Torrens Creek over 250 mile away. The river goes down to Longreach, Stonehenge and Windorah, and hooks up with the Barcoo River near Jundah, then flows into the Cooper and, in exceptional flood years, makes its way into Lake Eyre in Central Australia. If you get big heavy rain at the headwaters, the water can rise and stretch out for six to ten miles in the flat open country. When it rained in Hughenden it would take a fortnight or more for the floodwaters to get to Stonehenge, over 300 mile away. It took about ten days for the water to go from Longreach to Stonehenge, travelling at about half a mile an hour; you hardly saw it shifting. When it was really slow, you could swim against the current in those floods and sometimes even beat it.

Driving the Buick through a water crossing on the way to Stonehenge, 1932.

We just knew that come December, when the storms came, we could be cut off for a couple of months. So about the end of November, Mum and Dad would send away for an order with Queensland Pastoral Supplies for three big bags of flour (as big as corn or jute wheat bags), a couple of bags of sugar, three or four great big tins of tea, a couple of cases of jam and a case of marmalade, two cases of tomato sauce and half a dozen tins of cream of tartar and bicarbonate of soda (we didn't have baking powder until much later). There'd be a carton of treacle, and a carton of golden syrup. We didn't order just one or two tins; everything was ordered by the carton. Our order would weigh at least a ton in total, and the orders for the big stations might have been over five ton. That was our standby during the flood; then usually by March you could go to town again, or Jim would finally get through.

If the river came up unexpectedly early, there could be tons of stuff that would normally come on the mail truck that instead had to be manhandled across the swollen Thomson River and the causeway between the two channels there. The council kept a heavy flat-bottomed steel boat on our side of the river that we could row out with. If it was out of the water you just about needed a draft horse to pull it in, but when the water came up high enough it would be floating there, tied to a coolabah tree; you'd swim out to it, hop in, untie it and row it to the bank, using a pair of oars stowed in the bottom of the boat.

At the river's edge we'd load the boat so it was right

down to the last few inches above the water, to avoid making too many trips. Although the water in the middle of the floods was usually very still and slow moving, we would be passing over the tops of trees, stumps and lignum bushes, and it was easy enough to get tipped over if you hit anything submerged, so we took our time and picked our way across.

When the water wasn't so high and had kept to its two main channels, which were a mile apart, we rowed across the first channel, then unloaded everything and loaded it all onto a two-wheeled trailer tied up to another coolabah tree. When the trailer was fully laden it could weigh a ton or more, and we all had to push it for a mile across this stone causeway. At the next flooded channel there was a suspension bridge with steel cables between two trees and with wooden slats. So we would pick up everything one by one, and put it on our shoulders and carry it across this bridge.

It was quite interesting going across the suspension bridge. It used to start moving up and down as soon as you started walking along it; if you didn't get in step with it, it would be coming up when you were coming down and it could kick you into the river, just like a springboard. You'd have a bag of sugar or mail or something on your shoulders or your back, and you had to walk like an emu in time with the bridge's movements. It was only about 30 yards in length, but I've seen people so scared of the bounce-up that they'd get down on their hands and knees and crawl across. As kids we saw it as great fun, and sometimes we would fall in purposely—but not with a bag of sugar. We also had to be extra careful with the bags of carbide for our lights. If the carbide got wet it would fizz and turn to gas, until it was all gone.

Suspension bridge over the second of the two main channels.

Chapter 4

The Depression

By 1932, when Australia was in the midst of the Great Depression, one of our neighbours had had enough of the isolation. He had a chat with Dad, and Dad agreed to swap Rosewood, the block he still owned down at Nyngan, for the block 40 mile from Red Knob which was called Beatrice Downs. Beatrice was slightly better country than Red Knob; it was stony country with stunted gidgee and boree trees, but it also had some patches of open downs where grass could grow better than in the ashy soil on Red Knob. Our soon-to-be-ex neighbour was happy to get a smaller place that was only 30 mile out of Nyngan instead of being 150 mile out on the Diamantina. He and Dad just swapped places; they probably swapped deeds, but no money changed hands that I know of. Dad now had two places in the Diamantina, Red Knob and Beatrice Downs.

The hut on Beatrice was less primitive than the one on Red Knob. It was a tin hut with a concrete floor, probably about fifteen by 25 foot (five by eight metres), and it was divided into three rooms. Dad built a cane-grass hut about 20 feet away from the tin hut, with a cane-grass walkway between the two. The cane grass was wonderful and cool; it kept most of the sun off. It certainly didn't keep out the rain, but then it didn't rain that often at Beatrice either— fourteen inches a year was the average, but it could get down to as little as four inches in a drought year.

Hugh, Arthur and Godfrey outside the original Beatrice Downs hut with Peter the goat in our homemade cart.

Dad put two great big bullock greenhides on the floor of the cane-grass shelter and Mum would throw a bucket of washing-up water over them early in the morning and they'd be damp and cool off, so you could lie on them in the heat of the afternoon. Of course, when you got up you used to smell a bit like greenhide, but you didn't mind.

At night us four boys slept under a small verandah in an old double bed, a 'stretcher' as we called it. It had four wooden folding legs which supported steel mesh with a mattress on top. The mattress was filled with cold lumpy coir, which is coconut fibre; it should have been washed and the fibre teased out each year, but it never was. We would sleep top to toe, but by morning the four of us would have slipped down to the middle of the bed, so you would wake up with someone's toes in your face.

The only water on Beatrice was about half a mile away from the huts and it had to be carted using the dray and water tank; we collected it in the same way as we had on Red Knob. Again, we didn't wash very much; even as we were growing up we used to use just one tub of water and then, when everyone had finished, it would be used for other purposes, like laying a little dust down or throwing over the bullock hides. There was no such thing as a garden; there wasn't the water for it. There was no running water through pipes and taps, nothing modern like that—it all had to be carried in buckets. We had one rainwater tank of 1000 gallons that collected any rainfall off the tin roof; that was only for drinking, no other purposes whatsoever.

It was still a hard life for Mum, but she did have a couple of little luxuries at Beatrice. Washing clothes had always started with three tubs—one great big tub, one medium and one small. Clothes used to go into the big tub first, to take off the majority of the dirt. Then they were wrung out and put into the next one for more cleaning, and finally into the little one. At Beatrice the clothes were then placed in a big copper, where they were boiled over a chip fire. I don't know why, but everyone boiled their clothes in those times.

As well as the copper, Mum now had a little stove in the tin hut; she very rarely cooked on the open fire after that, as all the cooking was done on this little stove. And last but not least, attached to the stove was a permanent hot-water fountain—a copper tank that sat on the very edge of the stove and could be filled with water, and had a tap on the bottom. Mum had instant hot—or at least warm (depending on the heat of the stove)—water on tap for the first time.

We only had carbide or kerosene lights back then. Carbide was a good light source but could be dangerous. It is a really hard stone—calcium carbide—and as I've mentioned you have to keep it perfectly dry until you want to use it, as it is extremely flammable and reactive with water. Carbide when added to oxygen gives you acetylene, which they use for cutting steel.

To use the carbide for lights, we'd put two or three pieces of it (about the size of hens' eggs) in a pint tin, and drip a few drops of water on the carbide, which would immediately start to fizz and form acetylene. We'd place over it another snug-fitting mug shaped tin, which had a tall thin pipe for the gas to come out of; a ceramic burner was attached to the end of the pipe. We'd wait for enough gas to form and move up the pipe, then light the burner directly. You'd light it up as it got dark and it would last you four to five hours; once it went out, you were left with a blob of wet white ash. It produces a beautiful strong white light, but it smells a bit like old socks. And if you haven't got gauze around your house or if you're out in a camp, all the moths come for miles and just try to fly straight at it.

We eventually switched to the kero lamps, as they were more convenient than the carbide—you could put a match to them straight away, you didn't need water to start them and they were easier to cart around. They stood about a foot high with a big long glass cylinder surrounding the flame. The light they emitted was terrible, though; it would maybe show you from door to door and that was about it.

No electricity meant no refrigeration, of course, but we did have a couple of Coolgardie 'safes' (or coolers) at Beatrice. The first one had wire mesh around a big wooden frame with a tin dish filled with water on the top and hessian bags down the sides. Strips of felt or flannel went from the tray down onto the sides and they sucked water out of the tray on the top and dripped down the hessian to keep it moist. Any air blowing through the hessian would keep things reasonably cool inside.

The other type of Coolgardie safe we had, used charcoal as an insulator to keep things cool. It was made of a big box, six foot high, with a smaller box inside, and we would fill the space between the boxes with chunks of homemade charcoal. Water was poured over the top of the charcoal; as it dripped down, the inner box would become cold. The charcoal cooler needed water running through it all the time, and it was a bit of a problem carting water for it, but it kept things much colder than the first safe. At Connemara Station they apparently had a cold room—a small room completely lined with a layer of charcoal, with a walk-in door—and that must have been really something.

Another problem with the charcoal cooler was that we had to make our own charcoal to put in it. We would help Dad dig a big hole in the ground, say six foot long and four foot deep, and get a load of wood—coolabah was the best. We'd put it in the bottom of the hole and start a fire. When we got it really roaring and all the logs were well alight, we'd cover it over with a sheet of tin and then cover that with dirt to smother the flames. In a week to ten days' time we'd go back and dig it all out. It was a dirty black job, but we used that charcoal for the cooler as well as for the forge, where we repaired plough shears, fixed crowbars, or did other metal repairs.

Dad had an anvil and a forge under a tree, and everything had to be made and repaired using our homemade charcoal as fuel. We rarely made horseshoes; Dad didn't shoe the horses if he could help it, not even our draft horses—the iron for the horseshoes was too expensive. He always kept the hooves trimmed and looked after, because a horse is useless without good feet. Some of the saddle horses were shod on the front hooves, but very rarely on the back. When those shoes became worn down, Dad would put them in the forge, straighten them out, make them thicker and reuse them. Nothing was ever wasted.

During the Depression years of the early 1930s my brothers and I were just kids, we didn't know there was a depression on or what it meant. We didn't have any money, but neither did anyone else. On top of that, we were a long way from anywhere, and there weren't many tramps or 'swaggies' out there, unlike other parts of Australia during the Depression. We were too far away.

I remember seeing swaggies only a few times, mostly when we were travelling to Longreach or visiting a larger property. These men would try and find work on farms and in towns they travelled through; if there wasn't any permanent work available—which was usually the case—the cockies would often provide food and shelter in return for some menial job like cutting wood for the house stove.

It was a little bit easier for the swaggies in the outback than in the bigger towns, where there were more people looking for work. They'd get to a station after travelling 20 or 30 mile between places, and they used to get a couple of feeds and generally something for a day's work; then they'd get their tuckerbag filled with a bit of tea and sugar and some meat—meat didn't cost anything so it was nothing to give it to someone down on their luck—and away they'd go. Sometimes they'd be able to pick up a bit of work when shearing was on; for us, that was the busiest time of the year.

Chapter 5

Shearing at Beatrice

RED KNOB AND Beatrice were run in conjunction with each other. To begin with there was no shearing shed on Beatrice Downs, but it was a better block. It was rated one sheep to every six acres, marginally better than Red Knob; but even then we used to get a pretty good drought every three or four years.

Dad built a shearing shed there out of bush timber, with a tin roof to catch the rainwater. The shed had four stands—a stand is the space where the shearer shears, with a chute to let the sheep out afterwards. Dad built everything himself because there was no money to pay someone else; this was right in the heart of the Great Depression, but the sheep still had to be shorn, depression or no depression.

The shearers used to arrive on Beatrice in winter; we always started shearing in July, the middle of the winter dry season. The whole lot of them'd arrive on the back of a three-ton truck—shearers, classer and presser, and everything needed for a month or more of shearing. They'd be away from towns for long periods of time, so all their supplies would be perched up on the back of the truck.

They brought all their provisions, even bales of straw to stuff their own mattresses with. The owners supplied calico mattress covers, and the shearers stuffed straw or hay into them when they arrived, then sewed them up. There were no quarters whatsoever on the small selections back then, so the men had to put up their own tents; usually the place supplied the poles to throw the canvas over, but that was all.

Everyone was very sparing with water. They used to get most of their drinking water from our 1000-gallon rainwater tank at the house, because usually by that time of year the dams and waterhole were getting pretty low and the water was usually a bit smelly.

They used to have to rig up a homemade shower using a four-gallon petrol can hoisted up and with a little self-stopping plug on a string in the bottom. They weren't allowed four gallons of water, of course—I think it was only about a gallon or two. They'd let out enough water just to wet themselves, stop the water with the plug, lather themselves with soap, then pull the plug again and hold onto the string as they washed the soap off. Some of them had coppers or kerosene tins to warm the water in winter, but they had to do that themselves—it wasn't up to the station owner to provide hot water.

We did have to provide dunnies for the shearers, so we used to dig a trench about ten foot long and two foot wide. The depth of the hole depended on how long you thought shearing was going to continue for—if it was expected to take a month, the hole had to be at least three foot deep. Every day the dirt that had originally been dug out went back into the trench in a layer to cover the sewage, and to try and keep the fly numbers down. At each end we'd put in a large forked stick, about sixteen inches off the ground, and on that stick rested a fairly substantial rail for them to sit on. As kids we thought it was quite a funny sight to see four or five shearers sitting on this rail at the one time, like crows on a branch.

When shearing was over, the shearers would move on to the next place and the wool would be carted away, initially on horse-drawn wagons, and then, in later years, by truck.

Working in a shearing shed is good hard work. Other than the shearers, the most important bloke in the shed, as far as the cocky is concerned, is the classer—he can make or break you. His job is to assess the wool and class it according to its strength, fineness, colour, length, and how much vegetable matter is caught in it. If he makes a mistake, it can cost the owner a lot of money; for example, if he puts one bad fleece in a line of AAAM fleece (the code for the best line of merino wool), then the whole line can be downgraded and the cocky is paid less. A line of wool can compose of three or more bales of the same type or class of fleece. Years ago they just opened a bale on the floor and, if there was one bad fleece, it could downgrade the entire line; now they class the line through many samples. The classer is also usually the boss of the shed.

The roustabout folds and picks up the fleece off the board, the area encompassing and directly in front of all the shearer stands, in one go, before throwing it out onto the classing table for the wool roller and classer. He then sweeps the board clean while the shearers catch another sheep.

Back then, if you had a fairly big shed—anything over six shearers—you'd have a penner-up person as well, and he used to keep the sheep up to the shearers, filling the pens behind each shearer with fresh woolly sheep. When you got down to the last few in the pen, they would be the harder sheep to shear. Shearers pick the best sheep to shear first, so the penner wasn't allowed to put any more sheep in when the shearer yells out 'Sheepo!', until there was only two or three left in a pen, otherwise you'd end up with a whole lot of what they call 'snobs' or hard sheep to shear. Sometimes the penner would also help the boss with the sheep outside the shed or shifting the bales out of the way or other odd jobs.

When the wool is first thrown on the table, all the little hard bits of old dung and the shorter cuts of wool tend to fall through the slats on top of the wool table. The wool with vegetable matter or dung in it is put in a separate bin.

If the shed had more than six stands, you'd often have a wool roller working on the table with the classer. His job was simply to 'skirt'—to take off the edges, the legs, the bit down the brisket (the chest) and the breech (the backside), because these parts can be filled with vegetable matter, grass seeds and dried vegetation. Years ago there would be a piece picker whose job was to go through those sections again, picking the good wool out of the hard wool, but now it's all just thrown into one bin, so that's done away with one man. Nowadays, especially in smaller sheds, in addition to picking up and throwing the fleece, the roustabouts may also help to skirt the wool, which does away with the wool roller as well.

The fleece is thrown down with the dirty side up, and as you skirt the fleece you throw the edges into the middle so the clean side shows, so by the time you're finished it's all nice and white and in a bundle. Whenever you work all day on fleeces, your hands become lovely and soft from all the lanolin coming out of the wool, but then you have to be careful of dried thistles and spiky weeds around the brisket and skirt getting into your softened skin.

The classer then comes along and classes the wool. You might have four thousand ewes in one mob, and there could be six to eight different classes of wool in that mob. But if the sheep have been properly classed into mobs according to their wool before the shearing begins, there might only be three or four classes. When you have over three bales containing a single class, you have a line of wool. It's better to get bigger lines of wool as the buyers don't like buying many different small lots. Small lots are called star lines.

Once the wool has been classed, it's placed into the bin for that class and the presser then compacts this wool into bales. The presser is a specialist and he's the hardest-working member of the team, especially before the electric press was brought in in the 1950s. If he's got a lot of shearers shearing and they're doing a lot of sheep, he is really working. He gets paid not by the bale but by the weight he presses—per hundredweight it used to be, meaning 112 pounds, but now it would be per 100 kilos.

In a really big shed—I'm talking forty to a hundred stands—there would also be a man who weighed the bales and branded them with a stencil. But I haven't seen a working shed with more than twenty stands for over forty years. Once you got over twenty shearers, it was a big shed, but all those big sheds are gone.

In 1956 in Queensland there were still big sheds being run because they were big places running sheep, some shearing over two hundred thousand head. Nowadays there are still large numbers being shorn, not as many as back then, and they are shorn more efficiently and with fewer men, all doing multiple jobs. There are not many sheds over six stands now.

These days, there are no real rules in the shed, but in the past the rules around work hours were very strict. Because of union involvement in Australia from the 1890s, agreements were put in place between shearers and wool producers—the graziers—which were strictly adhered to. Up until 1915, shearers worked a nine-hour day, but on a lot of places, especially in winter with shorter days, you couldn't shear that long—there were no lights in the sheds and the shearers couldn't see to work. But from 1915, when it became an eight-hour day, shearing starts at 7.30 a.m.; they shear for a two-hour 'run' and break at nine thirty, start again at ten and work through to twelve, then start up again at one in the afternoon and shear two more runs, with a break in between, before knocking off at five thirty. Three minutes before the time to knock off, they'd ring the bell, and that gave the shearer, if he'd caught a sheep three minutes before, time to finish by the end of the run. The roustabout could still have the wool on the table that had to be classed, but the shearer had to stop. You weren't allowed to go into a pen to catch a sheep after the bell went; you weren't even allowed to stand with your hand on the door before the bell rang again at the start of a run—that was how strict the rules were. You didn't work overtime.

Now, of course, there might be half a dozen sheep left to shear at five thirty in the afternoon and so the shearers will do them. You couldn't do that back then—even if it was last thing on a Friday, you had to come back on Monday morning to shear them and you might have missed a bloomin' good run, to the annoyance of the grazier who would have to keep the last few unshorn sheep fed and watered around the shed over the weekend.

Chapter 6

Going droving

AFTER SHEARING EACH year at Beatrice, we'd take the sheep over to Red Knob for three or four months, and they'd only come back to Beatrice for crutching—removing the wool around the sheep's tail and breech, to keep the flies out before the wet season. Dad had to stop over at Red Knob with the sheep because of the dingo problem.

Whenever we ran out of feed for the sheep, or even if we just had to move animals between Red Knob and Beatrice, we'd take the sheep on the road and go droving on horseback. Droving trips happened all the time, and we'd have to camp out with our animals.

The first memory I have of droving was when I was about five and I went along to help Dad and Arthur. I had a very quiet, very high horse. It was a long way up for a little kid. To get on him, I used to have to put him alongside a tree or fence or stand him in a gully. We didn't have any saddles—Dad didn't believe in saddles for kids. We were never allowed to use stirrups, even when we were older kids and started to use saddles, for fear that we would get hung up by them. Being hung up in the saddle is horrible—it's when your boot, shoe or even your foot gets stuck in the stirrup when you're unseated. The horse will usually run off, dragging the rider along by the trapped foot. Thankfully, it never happened to me as a child.

At the age of five I sat on a soft sheepskin with a surcingle, which was a strip of leather like a thick belt that went around the horse's belly to hold the sheepskin in place rather than a saddle and stirrups.

I remember one day on that trip, and I don't know how it happened, but the sheep got away from us. It was a great big mob and they got onto a bit of green pick and took off everywhere, spreading out. There weren't enough of us to contain them. As Dad and Arthur went off to gather them up, Dad told me to stay at the back of the mob. I was left there alone, riding this big old horse back and forth behind the sheep to keep them moving forward, and it was starting to get dark and I couldn't see anybody. I started to worry—they seemed to have been gone for so long—and I began to cry, believing I'd never see anybody again. Finally Dad and Arthur came back with the rest of the sheep in a mob. I pretended that I had been very brave.

We were always given jobs, even when we were five or six; actually you don't have to be very bright to ride along behind a mob with somebody telling you what to do. And it did help Dad out.

About 50 mile from Beatrice was the Longreach stock route; in the drier winter months there would be large numbers of livestock and their drovers heading south-west along that route. Putting large numbers of stock on trucks was unheard of back then—there was no such thing as livestock trucks or road trains, and animals had to be transported long distances via the railways, and then walked along stock routes.

The drovers used to bring a lot of cattle in from the Northern Territory and put them on the Longreach stock route. They would come in from Winton or unload off trains at Longreach and they'd go into the channel country to the west of us—down along the Thomson River, down to Galway Downs, Keeroongooloo, Thylungra, Booloo Downs, or even down further, eventually transporting them out at Quilpie on the train to the meatworks and markets in Brisbane, which was about just over 600 mile or about 1000 kilometres away, in almost a straight line.

The sheep and cattle would start to arrive after the wet season had finished and the river had gone down, say at the end of March or early April. There could be thousands of cattle heading down the river with their drovers, each mob about ten mile apart, which was the usual distance they would travel in one day. Most of these mobs had a thousand to thirteen hundred head in each. In among these mobs of cattle there would also be mobs of sheep, anything from five thousand to fifteen thousand head of sheep all travelling in the same direction, a day's travel apart.

We rarely saw them ourselves, but the people living along the stock route would see the drovers and their stock coming through. Most of the stock routes weren't fenced, and some were over a mile wide running through large paddocks. The larger stations generally had a man watching out at those times. Although droving stock were generally kept moving in one direction, they could still fan out to graze along the way. If the property owners had stock running in the channels, they had to keep them out of the way of the drovers, or their own stock might not be in the paddock when they mustered next—they might have joined up with a droving mob.

In the harder, drier country in all those Vergemont channels there were big claypans. Some were very large indeed—two, three, some of them five mile long—and absolutely dead flat, not a blade of grass on them. When it rained, the water used to run off them like it was coming off a roof. On the edges of the claypans there were little gullies with bluebush swamps in them where the animals could water.

The bluebush was three or four foot high; when the wet season came, the swamps would fill up quickly and the brolgas would nest in or around them, and there would suddenly be millions and millions of frogs—you could pick up a hatful of tadpoles and frogs just by scooping up some water to drink. The frogs must have been buried down in the mud during the dry season, because they couldn't possibly get there any other way. The brolgas were a great turnout with their flamboyant dancing and mating displays. There used to be a lot of carpet snakes along those creeks and swamps as well, but I haven't seen a carpet snake in the wild now for forty years. The bluebush swamps have all but disappeared too, as overgrazing filled them with silt. Obviously the carpet snakes, brolgas and frogs have disappeared along with them.

Sometimes when you looked across the paddocks out there, it didn't look like there was much grass; the ground just seemed to be covered in big stones. But to see if you've got a drought, you don't look at the country, you look at the sheep.

There were plenty of native grasses growing there: para-keelya, tarvine, bindi-eye, potato vine and button grass. They didn't look like much, but they would carry sheep through. Mitchell and Flinders were the two main grasses you found in our country, but they often competed with each other. Mitchell was the main native grass and it grows after summer rain—if you have Mitchell grass, you're going to have a good season. Flinders grass only grows about a foot high, and it's a really good soft grass, a lot softer and easier for the sheep to digest than Mitchell grass. Stock just love it, especially as it hays off, but once it gets wet, it turns into a black mat on the ground and the stock won't touch it, so you don't want any rain in winter.

Usually we had storms in December, sometimes earlier. If you had green feed at Christmas it was unusual, and you were lucky. Good rains always brought the birds. We used to get flock pigeons, thousands of them. They looked like a homing pigeon but a bit smaller, and all the one browny colour. I haven't seen one of those since 1950.

There were plenty of emus; they weren't much of a problem, although they were often blamed for breaking fences. They'd try and hop over them—they'd put their feet through, but then they could get hung up and stuck, and you'd find them dead much later, still caught up in the fence. We caught a young emu one time and I said to the jackaroo who was with me, 'If you ever want to make a pet of them, you put them down your shirt. You'll never get rid of them, they'll follow you everywhere.' But I didn't tell him that they 'shit like a pet emu', an expression used out there that certainly rings true. He put the emu chick in his shirt and for the rest of the day he well and truly smelt like a pet emu.

They do make good loyal pets, but they're a bloomin' nuisance—anything shiny they'll pick up and eat. Same with a pet brolga. If they were hanging around when you were fixing something, you'd be inclined to lose screws and anything small and shiny—they'd grab and swallow them before you could stop them. Then you'd have to put them in a cage overnight so you could retrieve the missing parts when they passed through them.

When the button grass dried off in April, we'd get flocks of thousands of budgerigars come through. When button grass seed falls out, the sheep will feed on it like corn, and the budgies love it too. You would see a cloud of green and yellow as they came in. There weren't many trees out there, so they'd nest anywhere there was a depression or hollow— in the fork of a tree, on top of a fence post. They were only around when the button grass went to seed and then they'd disappear again. Where they'd come from and where they went I wouldn't know.

There was an old story I heard from the early 1900s, about a young bloke hired as a stockman out at Terrick Terrick Station, south-west of Blackall. He was passing a tree and heard some young galahs in its hollow, fifteen foot off the ground. Perhaps he decided to try and collect a baby galah as a pet, as he stood on the back of the quiet old horse he'd been riding, reached up and put his hand down into the nest in the hollow of the tree. At that moment his horse put its head down and stepped away, probably to feed, and left this bloke hanging there, the weight of his body trapping him. Because his horse had moved away, the bloke couldn't get his arm out. In desperation he got out his pocketknife and tried to cut off his arm at the shoulder, but he couldn't do it. He managed to cut it off at the elbow and fell from the tree; he walked a few feet and then collapsed.

When he didn't return to the station, they sent out a search party and found his dead body at the foot of the tree. His forearm was still up in the tree. They had a lot of trouble getting it out of that hollow, and they found the birds' nest when they were removing it. They buried the arm alongside him at the base of the tree.

Some things you just don't do by yourself out there, but he was only young, I guess.

Chapter 7

Digging tanks

MY SISTER ETHEL Constance was born in 1932, just after we moved to Beatrice, two years after Lach, and so there was a little girl to join us rowdy bunch of boys. Mum now had five children under eight years of age.

As I've said, water was a priority on Beatrice. Because we didn't have any money to pay contractors to put a bore down into the Artesian Basin as some of the big stations did, Dad dug out big dams, or 'tanks' as they're sometimes called out west. He used draft horses drawing three-quarter-yard Gaston scoops, and employed three local brothers to run a team each to help dig out the dam as quickly as possible. It was a very slow process, especially digging the 24,000-cubic-yard (18,350-cubic-metre) dam, which was the biggest we put down. It could take months, sometimes years.

Up till the 1950s, all of our dams were put down with draft horses. One team of horses dug up the earth in front of the scoop team using a single mouldboard plough. When the scoop was full, the scoop team of horses would drag it away to be emptied. The horses walked six abreast with these ride-on scoops, which were fairly modern at the time—it was quite a luxury for us, not having to walk alongside the scoop day after day.

Digging out a dam at Beatrice with horse-drawn ploughs and Gaston scoops. Only half the dam was built at a time so the horses always had water.

We had about thirty draft horses to pull these Gaston scoops, and ten or twelve saddle horses. I didn't like horses, especially draft horses—I hated the coots of things. Everything about them was just hard work. Arthur and I would often have the job of mustering the horses in for Dad, getting them in before sunrise every morning—that was quite a feat in itself. The paddocks we let the horses out in at night could be as big as 15,000 acres. Even catching the saddle horses in the smaller, 1000-acre paddock at Beatrice could still be hard in the predawn light.

We never hobbled the draft horses; we used to put bells around their neck instead. Horses form their own little groups that always run together, so we'd put a bell on one of the horses in each group, and even in the dark at four or five in the morning we could locate the ones we wanted by using the sound of the bells. Sometimes we'd have to get them all in, but generally the bells saved time if we only wanted one or two teams; I have always liked the sound of a bell, ever since.

We usually had to have four goats milked and the horses into the yard by shortly after sunrise. Sometimes you'd sneak a bit longer in bed than that, but not on those busy days when the dams were being put in. Arthur and I some-times used to cook breakfast—chops, rissoles, eggs—ready for when everyone else got up.

You didn't have to go and get the goats, as they used to come home by themselves in the afternoon after grazing out in the paddocks all day. Mum would lock the young goats away from their mums at night; in the morning, after getting the horses in, we'd milk the nannies and then let them back out with their kids. The good thing about the goats was that you could eat their meat and even make butter out of their milk. Mum would warm the milk up on the stove in a washbasin, lift the cream off the top and make butter out of it. The cream is real white and the butter is also white—you don't get yellow butter with goats. Goats don't get layers of fat on them like sheep either. I suppose you get used to goat butter, but it does taste a bit goaty—it tastes just like they smell.

We'd start yoking up the horses at sunrise, which took the best part of an hour; because they were working six abreast it was a bit easier for them and we used to work them all day. Then at least an hour before sundown they had to be taken back to water and unyoked, so the sweat could dry on them before the temperature dropped at night. You always had to water them first because sometimes they'd start feeding straight away and not go to water. If that happened, the next day they'd be all tucked up and unable to work. By the time we got back home ourselves, it would be around nine o'clock. They were long days—four o'clock in the morning through to nine o'clock at night, six days a week.

Funnily enough, the main problem with digging dams in this way could be the water. With the horses, unless you had water within a few miles, it was too much walking for them. So if the weather had been very dry we'd build a small waterhole and wait for it to be filled by rain before we started dam sinking. Then we'd start on half the dam, going as deep as we could, then leave the dam until it rained and hope that it would fill up with water. After rain we'd start on the other side of the dam, digging deeper than the first half and then draining the water into the part we'd just built; then we'd gravitate the water from one side to the other as we worked, so the horses would have water all the time. Mostly, though, we just had to dig dams in good seasons, when there was plenty of water already in the waterholes.

Dad was a tough sort of a man. He was very tough physically—he'd grown up in a tough area, and gone to a tough school, which he didn't attend for long, and he sort of expected that everyone else should be as tough as he was. He wasn't only tough physically, he was also tough mentally.

Poor old Mum, we used to feel sorry for her sometimes. But I don't think she knew any better, and she loved him. She used to protect us a bit from Dad, as he was strict with discipline. I don't think he was unfair—he listened to an argument if you put one forward, but it had better be good. Most importantly, you couldn't tell a fib—if you told a lie, then you'd cop it.

As four energetic boys, we'd often have a bit of a donnybrook between ourselves. We generally all got on very well, but every couple of months there'd be a bit of an argument and Dad would grab one of us, whoever he thought was the cause of it, and he'd give us a bit of a touch up. Mostly it wasn't that bad, and we probably deserved it. And if we got too boisterous, Mum could always bring out the castor oil.

One time when Dad was sinking one of the tanks, he was thrown out of the scoop when it hit a stone and he landed on the traces, near where the horses were. He had a bad cut, over four inches long and an inch deep, right into the calf muscle of his leg. He tethered the draft horses, got on his saddle horse and rode the three mile home. Mum refused to touch it, so he sat down and stitched up his leg himself with an ordinary needle and thread, and then put this friar's balsam on it, which must have stung. How he did that—putting it onto a raw wound—I'll never know. He then put on a bandage, got on his horse and rode back to work. He was tough.

You were in danger whenever you were badly hurt on one of those isolated places. I remember one time when our neighbour Bill Springer at Thurles Park was putting down a dam with horses about the same time as us. He had a round yard that he used to put the horses in every morning at sunrise—it was a holding yard really, with just one steel wire around the top of some rough-hewn posts. This bloke was breaking in a horse for Mr Springer in that yard when the horse bucked and he went up in the air and came down on his stomach on one of the wooden posts. The post was about as wide as a hen's egg, or a bit bigger, but it had a bit of a sharp point on it, because it's easier to cut a post from a sapling at an angle, rather than straight across. Here he was impaled on the post, and the blokes who were working with him had to lift him up to get him off. If he'd been out there by himself, he wouldn't have been able to get off.

They brought him over to our place in Mr Springer's tiny little Austin 10, because they knew they could get him to Longreach quicker in Dad's Buick than in that little car. I was only a kid at the time, and I remember seeing the gaping wound as a couple of blokes lifted him onto the kitchen table. There wasn't much blood, strangely enough, and it didn't burst his bowel, otherwise he'd probably still be hanging on the post. Even in the Buick, it took them about eight hours to get him to the hospital in Longreach; five or six hours driving down rough roads, with at least twenty gates to stop and open and close. Still, he recovered and was back in a few weeks.

Out there, you either got better or you died. There are a lot of graves out west to pay testament to that, and a lot of blokes who lasted till they were ninety years. The ones that got better survived. But the other poor buggers are buried out there.

Chapter 8

Boys will be boys

BRIAN ROBERT WAS born in 1934, another boy to keep Mum busy.

By then I was about eight, and one of the jobs we had was collecting 'dead wool'—going out and collecting the wool off the carcasses of any sheep that had died during the year. Sometimes they might have nearly a full year of wool growth on them when they died, and it would be a waste to leave the wool out in the paddock. We used to go out with our horses, with a bag over the pommel of the saddle, to where we'd previously seen a carcass, and fill our bags with the dead wool. The grubs and such ate nearly all the skin and carcass over about six months, so just the wool and bones would be left there, with a whole lot of dry maggot shells. We'd leave it as long as possible so the smell wouldn't be too bad.

The timing for collecting the wool depended on whether the sheep had died in summer or winter; once the flies got into it, especially after the summer rains it would be a maggoty mess, or if it was a damp you had to wait for it to dry out. You can collect the wool straight after they die, if you get to it within two days before the flies; you scrape it straight off the dead sheep's rotten skin, but it's smelly. The wool looks clean—it could have been shorn for all anyone knew, except for the smell.

If we came across a carcass that was still full of live maggots, we'd sometimes throw it up into a tree; over time all the bones and flesh would fall out and just leave the wool in the tree. It was quite good money for us kids as Dad would give us the money for the dead wool we collected.

Collecting dead wool in hessian bags on a pack horse.

*

Mum and Dad used to have to go to town now and again. I remember one particular day when our neighbour Bill Springer went with them. I don't know why they didn't take us four older boys with them—we might have been a handful.

Mr Springer drove over to Beatrice and left his little Austin 10 utility at our house. It was about a 1930 model, with a canvas hood, and it wasn't much bigger than a pram—it was the smallest car you could ever imagine, with only a ten-horsepower engine, and I've never seen one since. It could carry about two people in the front, and two kangaroo carcasses on the little utility tray at the back. I've seen plenty of push mowers with more horsepower than it had.

He left it at our place with four young boys, so we taught ourselves how to drive. It had a three-speed manual gearbox on the floor but was otherwise similar to driving the Model T. We went out on a claypan near our house and drove it around and around, hour after hour, until it nearly ran out of petrol. When we came back we filled it up from Dad's petrol supply. But we were also worried because there were all of these tracks round the house, and we knew if Dad saw them he'd soon figure out what we'd been up to. We'd seen in the cowboy movies how to cover tracks, so we got our horses and tied branches to their tails and rode them round and round, dragging the branches through the dust to cover up all of these tyre tracks. When Dad got home, all he saw was hundreds of strange hoof prints; he asked us what the heck we'd been up to and we just told him we'd been playing Cowboys and Indians. Nobody knew until many years after.

Bill Springer's mum used to own a pub in Longreach but had long since retired to a house in the town. On our trips to town we often stayed with her instead of camping on Gin Creek. Mrs Springer could be a bit uppity, and she was having a bit of a row with a bloke by the name of Lionel Steadman, who ran the night cart. There was no town sewerage in Longreach then; all the houses backed onto a laneway, with the outdoor dunnies against the back fence, at least twenty yards from the house. The night cart was an ordinary light wagon pulled by two horses that collected the night soil (the dunny waste) first thing every morning. This Steadman would work on one side of the lane and his offsider would work on the other, collecting the cans from under the dunnies, putting a lid on them, loading them into the night cart and replacing them with clean ones. The council hired the night cart to collect the town's waste, take it out of town and dispose of it.

Steadman and Mrs Springer didn't get on—she had previously roused on him about something or other—and one day he must have decided to get his own back. He saw her going for her life down the path towards the toilet just as he was about to open the back door and empty the can. She came down the path, flat out, and just before she got to the door, he opened the back door into the dunny to remove the pan and yelled out, 'Hold it, Mrs Springer!' Then he replaced the can and yelled out, 'Righto, you can let it go now!'

Mrs Springer was mortified. She would have probably been the only one in the street with a telephone, and she went in and rang the shire clerk to complain about Steadman's ungentlemanly manner. One of the clerk's henchmen rode his pushbike down—there were no cars for staff at that time—and he told Steadman, 'You're sacked!' Steadman said, 'You can't sack me,' and the shire bloke said, 'Well, I am sacking you—you get!' To which Steadman replied with a smirk, 'You can't sack me. See those two horses out there? They belong to me. See that night cart? I own that too. You know, if I leave here, there will be nobody to cart your shit,' and told *him* to get. The shire bloke climbed back on his bike rather meekly and left.

As kids we were fascinated by this Steadman and his horses. He would call out 'Yeeep' and the horses would walk on, and when he'd call 'Whoooap' they'd stop at the next place. We'd try to use the same calls on the horses, but they wouldn't shift and wouldn't stop for us. They only responded to his voice.

Steadman delivered the waste out to where three Chinese families lived, three mile out of Longreach on the western side. Every day the Chinese families would dig a big long trench and they'd go along with the cans and put the night waste into it. Someone would then come along behind them and fill it over and mix it in with the dirt they'd dug out. Next day there were cabbages and lettuces growing there.

That's what they did in China, and so that's what they did in Longreach.

Every morning and evening those same laneways at the back of the houses in Longreach would serve as a goat highway, for up to five thousand goats. All the western towns in outback Queensland had nanny goats for fresh milk. The goats went out to graze and then returned to their own yards at night. Occasionally you'd have to go and sort them out, but most of the time they knew which house they belonged to.

There was a big town common, about 10,000 acres, and once or twice a year the council would muster all of the goats into a pound. Council owned a special sort of milking billy goat, a Swiss breed called a Saanen, that would breed with all of the nanny goats. You paid the council a shilling to keep a milking goat, and they would put a numbered tin tag on a collar around the goat's neck; every year you'd have to pay another shilling per goat. Once the goats were six months of age you had to register them; otherwise, late in the afternoon of the muster day, any unregistered goats were kept in the pound while the rest were released. Anyone could go down and buy a nice little female kid goat for two shillings from the pound on muster days. You couldn't have a billy (male) goat over six months old. Billy goats over six months old had their throats cut after the muster, and if no one claimed them, the carcasses were sold for a shilling, or two shillings, depending on size. If you took a young nanny goat home from the muster, you had to keep it tied up and feed it for a week or so before letting it out, otherwise it would go back to its original home.

There was one tree in Mrs Steadman's street at that time and you didn't dare park your car underneath it. I remember someone once parked a four-seater sedan with a canvas hood under that tree to get some shade; a goat jumped up onto its roof to eat some leaves, and went through the canvas, its four legs down in the car and the rest of it stuck on top. Funniest thing we'd seen for a while.

Back at Beatrice, Arthur and I decided to rig up a flying fox between the cane-grass hut and the long-drop toilet near the chook house, about twenty yards behind the house. We made the flying fox from an old tyre on a rope attached to a pulley on a big steel cable. One end of the cable was tied to a large gidgee tree next to the house and was four foot off the ground; the toilet end was about fifteen feet high, and you had to climb up on top of the chook house to get on it and ride it all the way back to the house. We tied a knot in the cable about four foot back from the house, to stop the pulley before it hit the gidgee tree; when you came down at a fair rate of knots and saw you were getting close to the tree, you really hung on to the tyre, because otherwise you'd end up being shot straight out of the tyre and into the tree. It was terrific fun to whizz down to the house, but the younger boys weren't strong enough to pull it all the way up to the chook house themselves; only Arthur and I were strong enough for that.

One day I took the tyre up and tied it to the chook house while I went to the toilet. We always had a big stick near the dunny, because of snakes. Snakes were everywhere—they were mostly browns and yellow-bellied black snakes, plus a few carpets and little grass snakes and bandy-bandies. I don't know if there were any more of them then, but I was certainly scared of them as a kid. The stick was there in case any had slithered into the cool shade of the dunny to escape the heat.

The younger boys must have seen me take the flying fox up, or they just happened to see it tied up there. They would often try and sneak up, climb onto the chook house, get in the tyre and away they'd go—and I'd have to walk back home. Anyway, when I was sitting on the loo, I heard this rattling of the pulley block being moved. I raced out, pulling my pants up and waving this snake stick, but my brother Godfrey was already on his way. He had a bit of speed up by the time I came around the corner of the toilet, and I was chasing after him, yelling at him, and he was yelling for Mum.

Of course, he was looking back at me chasing him as the pulley block hit the knot, and it fired him into the tree and broke his nose. Mum heard the shouting and raced out in time to see me waving this stick and standing over her son, who had blood pouring out of his nose. I was yelling at him, telling him I was going to kill him. I hadn't touched him, but she thought I had destroyed one of her boys. So I got a hiding—well, the start of one, until I managed to scream out an explanation of what had happened.

We never really saw any other kids. Our nearest neighbours, the Springers, were twelve mile away and had no kids; Mr Springer had married late in life. Our horses were our playmates, and we'd go swimming with the horses in the dam to cool off whenever we could. The house dam wasn't very big, but it had about ten foot of water in it. We four older boys would go round and round in it, swimming with the horses. Ethel and Brian were a bit too young, but they joined us as soon as they could ride by themselves on a pony. Often horses will do 'woopsies', as we called them, as we rode them and us dirty little buggers would grab a handful of fresh horse dung and chuck it at each other. We were just boys having fun.

But as I learnt for myself later, you should never swim a mare. Most of the time, mares will swim, no problems, but a few old drovers had told us to never swim alongside a mare—just put the saddle on another horse and lead the mare. Don't know why they play up, but I had first-hand experience of that eventually as an adult.

Chapter 9

Learning to shear, and life's little luxuries

WE STARTED 'BARROWING' (learning to shear) virtually as soon as we could pull a sheep out of a pen. It was a requirement that all bush boys knew how to shear. Dad was a good blade shearer and, later, machine shearer; as soon as we were old enough to catch a sheep to be shorn, he taught us how to hold it, and how to shear with blades and a handpiece.

We started off crutching, but shearing took a little longer to master. When you shear a sheep, you pull it out of the pen and sit it up resting between your legs, and then you get hold of your handpiece. The mechanical handpiece operates a bit like hair clippers. You use the same handpiece whether you're left-handed or right-handed, but with a different set of combs on the end of it. The comb, with its many long teeth, is fixed to the base of the handpiece, and the three-toothed cutter is driven back and forth across the fixed comb at about two thousand revolutions per minute, cutting the wool picked up by the comb. The handpiece is attached to the overhead gear positioned above the shearer, that provides the power via shafts and joints so the shearer can move the handpiece around the sheep as he shears.

When you shear you start on the belly wool and keep it separate from the rest of the fleece, as it is often full of dirt and burrs. After removing the belly wool, you move the sheep over onto its right back leg, put your hand into its left flank and pull that back leg out so you can shear it. Then you shift your feet again and move the sheep into position against you and you make one blow straight up the neck, being careful not to hit the jugular vein—but that doesn't happen much, because shearers are careful there. After you do the first hind leg, you take off the top knot with one blow—that's the bit of wool that grows above the sheep's eyes, and if it grows too long the sheep can become 'wool blind'.

Next you do the neck and first shoulder, and you lie the sheep down and do the 'long blow' along the length of its spread-out body. When you start doing the long blow, the sheep is almost on its back, but it won't like being there for too long—as long as you keep a sheep moving they sit quietly, but if you try and keep them in the one place for very long they will often struggle.

You continue along the left-hand side of the sheep, then move your feet and the sheep so you have access to the right or 'whipping side', so called because of the shearing motion where you finish with a series of shorter blows running from the spine down towards the belly. Then you start up again at the head and gradually pull the head back so the sheep is sitting up again. When you finish, the sheep is almost sitting in the same position that it started in.

Finally, you turn and let it out the chute to wait outside in the counting-out pens, clean-shorn. You aim to take the most wool off in the shortest possible time and all in one piece, except of course for the belly wool and top knot. How you place your feet and move the sheep around is very important, but it all comes with practice and you gradually become a faster, cleaner and more efficient shearer.

By 1937, we'd built a new house at Beatrice Downs. It was quite a big house—four bedrooms, with floorboards, and enclosed with good windows and doors to keep out the worst of the dust and bugs, and a big verandah all around. Mum was always fastidious about cleaning—the floors had to be swept, then mopped with a rag soaked in O'Cedar oil, and then polished. All the old brass taps had to be polished, and even the kettle didn't escape a regular shine-up.

We didn't get water on to the house until 1938, when we put in a small windmill and we could pump dam water up to a high tank near the house, and after that we were able to have gravity-fed showers. It was still pretty hard to garden—you could garden in the wintertime sometimes when it was cooler, but not much in the summer. By the time the youngest brother was working, we had better water supplies and hot water—he was lucky. Arthur and I had the roughest time; Godfrey and Lach were alright, because we had a good water supply by then; and the younger two lived in the relative lap of luxury.

New homestead Beatrice Downs

Compared to Red Knob and the old hut on Beatrice, there were now lots of little luxuries. We got our first fridge in about 1938, a kerosene fridge. It worked well and was an improvement on the old safes; the major problem with kerosene fridges was that when the days got to 42 degrees Celsius, they started to smoke. If you weren't there to watch them, they'd catch fire, and the house would burn down. In the summer months we weren't game to leave the house on a really hot day, above 44 degrees.

Out there in summer, I've seen birds sitting in trees and it would be so hot that they'd just fall out of the tree dead. Crows and magpies would be standing with their mouths open and their wings lifted just off their bodies because of the heat; it wasn't very often that they'd die, but they could at 44 degrees and above.

Before we got our first refrigerator, we could only kill a small sheep during the summer months for fresh meat; it was only in winter that you'd kill a large steer or cow, then hang it in the trees (and later the meat house). The meat house was a hut separate from the house, it had a pitched roof made of spinifex, rather than tin, and gauze walls to keep out the flies. You could keep meat in it because it stayed cool. The spinifex that grows out there is a prickly-looking bush, like a porcupine; you can still find it out west of Roma. It starts off as a little bunch and gets bigger, and by the time the bunch gets to about ten foot wide, the centre dies and becomes hollow. It's very good for insulation. Beef was of course still salted and dried to keep it through the summer months.

At the new house we also had a Lister diesel generator that we'd run every second day and most nights for an hour to provide lighting. It wasn't very powerful; Mum could run an electric washing machine or the iron, but not both at the same time. With no toaster, we would still make our toast on the stove fire; we only had a wood fire in the main fireplace for about a month in winter.

We didn't have a telephone until 1940; before that the nearest telephone was at Warbreccan. Australian-invented Traeger pedal wirelesses were put in the outer stations like Connemara in the 1930s so the people out there could be in contact with a doctor or anyone with another wireless twenty-four hours a day. With the Traeger you sat on a chair with a pair of bike pedals screwed onto the floor attached to a generator, and you'd pedal like mad while you were talking; when you got knocked up, you'd give someone else a go by saying 'Over'. It was hard work but at least they were in contact with the outside world; they could call up other stations. If you were at Connemara, you'd get on and say into the mouthpiece, 'Connemara calling Diamantine Gates, over,' and then you'd stop pedalling and wait for them to respond. You only pedalled when you spoke, and you had to pedal fairly strongly but not fast; still, some of the women ended up with big muscles in their legs.

There used to be a medical session on the wireless between eight and nine every morning, where you could talk to a doctor and receive a consultation over the air. Before that there was an owners' session, where property owners could get on and discuss any issues they were having with water or fences, that sort of thing. After the medical session was a free-for-all, and then what was known as the 'galah' session for the ladies, where they could talk about cooking and babies and all the problems the ladies used to have. You'd hear them on the wireless getting breathless, and then they'd say, 'Over to you,' and the next one would start pedalling when they wanted to talk.

Talking about medical problems on the open radio used to be a bit embarrassing for some people. The doctor would consult his patient over the wireless, and everyone listening in could hear. The doctors would ask about the pain, how many times you'd been to the toilet, that sort of thing, and the whole district in a 500-mile radius would know that Mrs Brown had a stomach ache today or she hadn't had her period, and it was quite funny for a kid to hear. Some girls got into trouble; that didn't happen much—maybe they were too isolated—but if it was on the wireless, then everyone knew.

Still, it was a good service. After the Flying Doctor Service started up, most places had a great big Royal Flying Doctor Services chest. Each chest had a whole lot of drawers that were named and numbered, filled with different sorts of medicines (packets and bottles of pills), as well as antiseptic, bandages and Band-Aids. Rather than name the medication, the doctor would tell his patient over the wireless to take a certain number of pills out of, say, bottle number 26 at certain times of the day, to help with whatever was their ailment. As long as you could explain to the doctor what your symptoms were, you had reasonable access to medical and pharmaceutical help. You were better off than travelling all the way to hospital, unless you were really sick. It was a life-saving service really—if people needed further treatment, the doctor would suggest going to see a doctor, and if necessary going to hospital.

Years later we eventually put up a telephone line and tapped into the party line 36 mile away that was connected to Stonehenge. It worked most of the time, except when there was a windstorm or something like that and a branch would fall down on the line and break the connection.

With a party line, you would dial the line code for a neighbour on your line, or otherwise you had to go through the exchange to access another telephone on another line. The old phone box was a bit bigger than an A4 sheet of paper; it had a receiver on the left that you'd lift to connect. You wound the magneto on the phone which you could then ring—short and long, like Morse code—to contact someone on the same party line; if you wanted the exchange, it was just one long ring. Everybody had a different number or 'code'. Your number might have been 16S or 21B, with the number being your party line and the letter being Morse code. If you needed to access another line it was a trunk call; just about all of our calls were trunk calls, which meant they were charged by the minute.

There was often a mob of people with access to a party line. When there was a quick short ring, it signalled that whoever had been talking on the line was finished. Otherwise, whenever you picked up the receiver, you'd call out 'Working' to check if anyone was on the line.

If there was a certain nosy neighbour listening in, one of the callers might say something like 'Can you smell that?', and the other one would reply, 'Yeah, it's Mrs D's stinking feet.' Then there would be this indignant 'Indeed it's not!' and you'd hear a clunk as her receiver went down.

Mrs D was a bit of a battler out there. I don't know how many kids she had, but they all seemed to be running wild. Mrs D's old fella was a drover and he used to go away a lot, and she'd be at the house alone with the kids. The house was on the main road to Stonehenge, 100 mile down the river from Longreach. From her house she could see cars coming for miles and she'd race out and pull you up and ask, 'Can you go and get me a tin of milk formula?' When you returned, she'd run out to meet you, grab it and say, 'Thank you very much, that's very decent of you.' She never paid, of course, but you didn't really mind.

She used to smoke like billy-o—old Log Cabin tobacco, which you could get flake cut or fine cut. With a tin of fine cut, you'd gently tease out a small amount to roll a cigarette, sort of like steel wool. She'd often ask, 'You wouldn't have a smoke on you, eh?' Someone would hand their tin over to her and she'd have a paper ready and pull the tobacco up; as she talked, she'd keep pulling out more, and it would be going into her hand for later.

She had it tough, but a lot of people were the same.

Chapter 10

Real bad drought

NINETEEN THIRTY-EIGHT WAS a real bad drought year. We only had about four inches of rain for the whole year, compared to the average of fourteen, and they were useless, falling at the wrong time of year. Nineteen thirty-seven had been near as bad. We took off droving with over four thousand sheep—Dad, three of us older boys, and Alf Ballard, a local drover who used to come out and work with Dad every now and then. Because we didn't have enough horses, we needed to take it in turns riding, so one of us boys would have to walk.

We went out onto Farrars Creek and on to Connemara; Dad knew there was a good bore out there and plenty of low mulga for the sheep to eat. The manager at Connemara allowed us to come and cut whatever branches we needed off the mulga trees, as long as we didn't cut any of the high branches. This was so the trees would survive. We were actually feeding his cattle at the same time, so it suited him and it suited us.

Droving camp leaving Beatrice.

We were there for about three months, and our camp was fairly primitive. For shelter we had one big fly tent—a tarpaulin thrown over a rope tied between two trees and pegged out—and we lived under the mulga trees.

The sheep were being shepherded all the time. Each day we'd go out in a different direction—north, south, east, west. You never went the same way two days in a row. At night we'd put them in a Forest rope break, which was invented by a Longreach bloke, Jack Forest, in the 1920s. It was a five-strand Manila rope (made from hemp) with wooden break pegs that were about twenty feet apart. We'd create a circle around the sheep, or a half-moon shape if we didn't have enough rope for a circle.

We'd camp in the open half of the circle after the sheep were put in, then put our bedding down and tie the dogs up across the opening. The sheep would happily camp in the break for the night.

You drove the wooden pegs of the break into the ground when you set up; then, when you moved on, you pulled them out and rolled them up into a bag. They were then thrown on the back of your buckboard or wagonette, whatever you had. It needed to be easy—they were so light that one of us boys could roll it all up and handle it.

Mum used to come out to find us once a week or whenever she could, bringing something to eat, other than the corned meat we were living on. There was of course no refrigeration, so if you killed a sheep for meat, you only had fresh meat for the day and then everything remaining had to be salted.

Wherever we were, we salted nearly all of our meat to preserve it. When a bullock was killed at home in winter, we'd cut off what meat we could eat right then and that night hang the rest of it out in the trees; the next day we'd put it in corn bags and hang it back up, covered in salt, under the trees. After the first night, all of the blood and moisture would have run out of it, so it was a bit like South African biltong or American jerky. When you go to cook it, you soak it for half a day to get most of the salt out of it; then you tip out that first lot of water, cover it with water again and cook it. It's quite good actually, especially if you grew up with it; you learn to make all sorts of curries and stews.

We loved helping Dad—it was much better than boring schoolwork. We didn't do much schooling really—if there was any mustering or droving to be done, we had no option, we went to work. All the sheep were shifted between the places by walking, which took time, and we had no full-time employees. Schooling was just fitted in when we could manage it. We didn't care—schoolwork was always the last thing on our agenda. If we thought we could get away with it, we'd convince Dad that there was a dingo hanging around, or the boundary needed riding, and then we'd go to Mum and tell her, 'Dad says we need to do this.'

Our schoolwork was all done by correspondence, mailed out to us from Brisbane; it came out with Jim Doyle and the mail, so sometimes in a wet season we'd go six weeks or more without any new lessons arriving. If they knew the mail was going to be held up, they'd send you about a month's worth of papers. They sent out all the information for the lessons, plus exercise books, pencils and rulers. It was fairly basic.

At first Mum taught us. We learnt to write, neat copper-plate writing. I remember one correspondence lesson when we had to practise pages and pages of drawing perfect fishhook shapes for our letters. The fishhook shapes would then form the letter *m* or *n*, or be turned upside down to form the letter *u*. It was done over a period of time until it was perfect, and that was with maths as well—not a mistake was to be made.

We used to have to say our times tables over and over and Mum would hear us, and then suddenly she'd interrupt and ask, 'What's three times three?', that sort of business. If you wanted to, you got fairly good at figures. We only learnt four subjects—maths, English, geography and history.

Our first tutor was Mr Florence, an old retired school-teacher who wanted somewhere to live—we used to call him 'Gertie', because we thought he was a bit of an old woman, even though he was quite strict. The next year we had another ex-headmaster, a Mr Bone, and he was a very strict sort of bloke as well. They'd come out to live with us and do the job in return for a house to live in and somebody to cook for them.

Chapter 11

The mechanically minded one

I BROKE IN my first pony when I was about twelve. I used to watch the men break in horses and, when it came to it, just followed what they did. Dad was breaking in horses all the time, because other than driving the car to town, or carting gear in the Model T, everything was done by horse.

Like everyone out there, we bred our own horses. We had a draft-horse stallion, and Dad would sometimes trade horses with drovers going by. Horses were bought and sold, but you had to be careful—sometimes they could be stolen from 100 mile away.

As kids, we had our own ponies and old horses, and they helped us provide our own entertainment. On Sunday afternoons and on holidays we'd go running dingoes, chasing them on horseback; we'd get ten shillings per scalp for any dingo we ran down, so that was good sport. We could also get money for roo skins. That was our pocket money—we'd be paid for the roo skins when they were sold in Brisbane by skin dealers, and bounty money for the dingo scalps when we went into town.

Usually the big old buck kangaroos were slow and we could catch up with them on the flat pretty quick. We weren't allowed to have guns until we were older, so we'd race up beside them on our ponies and the idea was to hit them right between the ears with a waddy (a hefty piece of wood the size of a small club). The only problem was that after the buck kangaroo had been knocked up, he would sometimes stand up and try and grab at you. If this happened when you were at full gallop, you'd usually come off your horse and end up with a bit of skin off and a bloodied nose, and watch this old buck bound away. If we were in the stunted gidgee country, the buck would go in under low branches and the pony of course would follow; we'd get wiped off quite often, with another bloodied or broken nose the result. Then we had to go home and tell some fib about what had happened. We weren't going to tell Mum and Dad what we were really up to, they might think it too dangerous and ban us.

At one stage we worked out that these kangaroos were coming in to drink from the dam near the house after dark. They were coming in between a couple of big coolabah trees. Our idea was that one of us would get a torch and waddy, and we'd stand behind a tree and let the roo through; the boy with the torch would then shine the torch into the roo's eyes and, while he was blinded, the other boy would race in and grab him by the tail and hold him until the first boy hit him between the ears.

Being greedy, we wanted the biggest skins, so we went for the biggest roos. But when we had them by the tail, we weren't strong enough to hold them. The roo would head off across the claypan with one of us hanging onto the tail and the smaller boy running along beside with the torch, trying to keep up and massage the roo between the ears with the waddy. In the dark, of course, the bloke who was getting dragged along by the roo would be copping most of the blows on his back or arms. We thought the concept was brilliant, but in practice it was not recommended for two young boys.

When Dad thought we were old enough, he gave us our own guns. I would have been about thirteen when he gave me my first gun, an old Germen Mauser 9mm automatic pistol from the First World War. From then on I always took it out with me when we were working, strapped onto my saddle so it was easy to access.

Teenage kids just love guns. We learnt how to care for them mostly from visiting roo shooters. We used to get two or three camps of roo shooters a year coming out into that country after the skins. Anybody else who came along— shearers or anyone visiting—would want to have a look at what guns we had and have a chat about them. Guns were commonplace.

Our sister Ethel was involved in just about everything we boys did. Not to the extent of chasing roos, but as far as all the other pranks and things around the house, she was just another boy as far as we were concerned. We used to drive around in the Model T when we could get away with it and that was great fun, with all of us piled in. There were plenty of punctures on the rough rocky roads out there, so changing tyres was a frequent job. You'd seen someone else do it so often that when it happened to you as a kid, you knew what to do—it was just a matter of being observant.

You had to be a bush mechanic out there. Dad preferred horses, and my older brother Arthur didn't know the first thing about engines or anything mechanical—he had no interest in them. He preferred working the horses too, but I didn't like working with the draft horses—they were too slow. Being the mechanically minded one in the family, I used to do the work on the Model T and whatever else needed fixing. Nobody taught me about mechanics, and I didn't have the first idea to start with. But I just taught myself, and then my brothers who were interested learnt as well. To begin with, I would often fix things I thought didn't look right—pull it apart, see how it worked, put it back together, and it often went. Not always straight away, but it usually went in the end.

We were given an old 1918 Douglas motorbike that wouldn't go, and I thought I'd have a look at it. It was an unusual bike in that it had a V-shaped rubber belt drive. I managed to get it going; it was pretty slow and the V-shape of the belt would fill with dirt, but anyway it would get you from A to B. It was the silliest-looking thing, but I thought it was great. It was a good thing it didn't rain much out there, because you couldn't run that bike on wet grass or the belt would slip.

We had a Lister engine in the shearing shed at Beatrice and it never ran properly, so I pulled that apart and got it going. I don't know, I just love pulling something to pieces and getting it going again. As long as it's not electric—I won't touch electrical things. The spark in a modern car is electronic, so I couldn't fix that; but one time a magneto in one of the vehicles wasn't working properly, and yet I still pulled it apart and worked out how to fix it.

When I was thirteen I had to replace the bearings in the Model T. I think the model we had was called a 'Ton Truck', with little narrow wheels at the front, big ones at the back and a tray twice the size of an ordinary Toyota ute today. Towards the end of its life it had developed an oval crankshaft, so that if you went over fifteen mile an hour it would start to make a knocking sound and you knew you had done in the big end. It was my job to then replace the big end's bearings, which you could usually do in an hour or two. I waited for the wet season, when I had time to do more of the mechanical work, and made a start.

I had a four-gallon can sitting on the running board and I put all the bits into it, keeping them out of the dirt and dust. I pulled the sump plug out and all the oil ran out. I think there were about sixteen or twenty screws, and after I dropped the sump plate off, I had everything there to work with; I finished up within a couple of hours. You couldn't fix a modern car in that time. They were simple— great bushman's vehicles.

When I'd finished replacing the bearings, I couldn't get it started quick enough, so I didn't bother to wipe the grease off my hands. I cranked the crank handle, and it slipped in my greasy hands and came back and hit me fair in the mouth. It knocked one front tooth clean out, broke another off at the roots, broke one diagonally and another vertically—and that vertical break was the worst of them all for the pain.

Because the river was up, it was nearly two months before I could get to town, so Dad used a pair of pliers to pull out the tooth that was split vertically. By the time I made it to town, the whole lot of the top teeth, except a few at the back, were poisoned and had to be removed. So from the age of thirteen I had no upper front teeth. There have been a lot worse accidents out there, and you generally lie down if things get bad; but most things get better. There weren't too many things that would kill you.

Chapter 12

Boarding school

NINETEEN THIRTY-NINE WAS a bad year for Arthur and myself—Mum and Dad decided to send their two eldest boys to boarding school.

I was thirteen and Arthur was fifteen when we were sent to All Souls' School for boys in Charters Towers, 540 miles (900 kilometres) away. It used to take us three days to get to school. We would travel a day to get to Longreach, where Mum and Dad would put us on a train to Winton. We'd get off and spend the night at a pub in Winton, just the two of us, and get on another train the next day to Charters Towers, and arrive late the following afternoon.

I went away to school with a jagged mouth, looking like a bit of a thug after the accident with the Model T crank handle. I loved boxing, but there were no mouthguards then, so one hit in the mouth and there would be blood every- where. Especially for me, so I had to give that up quickly.

A dentist in Charters Towers eventually made a little plate to replace my very front upper teeth, but over time all my top teeth followed one another out, and I needed a complete top plate. The plate was just ordinary plastic; it was a bit rough and ready, and a yellowy colour, which was off-putting. I got really sick of those plates breaking, so I told the dentist I either wanted a rubber one, which would bend, or a steel one. Eventually I got a gum-coloured chrome-steel plate with the teeth coloured white, but during high school I had to put up with the plastic plates.

All Souls' was a church school and this old bastard, Canon O'Keefe, was the headmaster. He was absolute lord and master of the school, and he loved having that power. Once the teacher said, 'Quiet, please,' if you even whispered to someone, out you went to the front of the class, and bang, you'd get the cane. That was a shock. Another punishment was to make you stand out in the sun for three or four hours, or until you fell over. We quickly learnt that the best thing to do was to fall over as soon as you thought you could get away with it.

If you were sent to Canon O'Keefe for talking out of turn or for being late for class, he wouldn't even listen to you, even if you had some fair dinkum excuse—you had to put out your hand for a flick of the cane. If what you'd done was real bad or you'd been sent to him more than a couple of times, he had a leather strap that was two feet long that he used to double back; you had to bend over, and bang, the strap got you on the bum. It flicked just like a whip, so you got twice the speed at the end of it. That was worse than the cane.

It wasn't just two or three hits with Canon O'Keefe— he'd flog you and keep flogging you. It was sadistic, there was no doubt about it. After being caned I would be so sore I couldn't sit or stand properly, and I saw blood running down a boy's legs one time. The other masters, they didn't do anything about it. That principal at Charters Towers was a real Hitler.

We'd been raised without any religion or church-going – didn't even know what they were, and I had no time for what I learnt of it at school. Early on, I was caught getting out of religious instruction and was given a double dose of castor oil as punishment, but that was tame compared to what else was on offer. Later, Canon O'Keefe was trying to tell us about Christ being raised from the dead and how he flew up into the air, and about the Immaculate Conception, but there was no way in the world I was going to believe that! Being a bush kid I knew all about bulls and rams and horses, so I wasn't going to cop this stuff! Well, Canon O'Keefe reckoned he could flog it into me. I remember him telling us one day in religious instruction about Adam and Eve, and I told him they must have been inbred—bang again! It was my own fault, I suppose.

I think the caning at our school was par for the course in those days. They'd be put up before a judge and jury quick smart these days for the things they got away with back then. The Christian Brothers School was only about a mile away; on the few occasions we were allowed out, we would compare notes with the students there, and the brothers over there used to do the same sort of thing.

We might get out to the pictures once a term, but that was our only time out. And if you were caught off the school grounds at any other time, you were punished. If you misbehaved in any way, they could cut off all visitors, even your mother and father. They were cruel, emotionally and physically.

I was at All Souls' for twelve months, but after we went home for the Christmas break, I wouldn't go back. I told Mum and Dad, 'You can put me on the train, but I'll be hopping off at Winton or Hughenden or something.' I was just going to disappear. So they sent me to The Rockhampton Grammar School at Rockhampton. I had no problem there at all and I finished school a year later. I was the only one of us that went to Rocky. Arthur stuck it out at All Souls for the two years, but there was no way I was going back.

Canon O'Keefe tried to beat religion into me and failed. I tell everybody that that's why I don't go to church—'cause it was all belted out of me. I vowed I was going to kill him when I got big enough, but I never saw him again after I finished school. Probably a good thing.

The other boys spent a bit longer away at school than Arthur and me—Brian had four or five years away at school. The younger ones had a lot better education than us older boys, but we grew up during the Depression and the war, and we just had to come home and work. I didn't mind—after only two years, I'd had enough of school.

Chapter 13

MacFarlane Downs

IN 1940 DAD bought MacFarlane Downs at Tambo, about 220 mile (just over 350 kilometres) from Beatrice and Red Knob. It was 24,000 acres of better country but it was a badly rundown place with virtually no permanent water on it. I left school at the age of fifteen and a half, in the middle of the Second World War, and went straight home and worked—really worked hard—that first year at MacFarlane. I worked at least fourteen to fifteen hours a day.

We did a lot of weed-control work. There was about 10,000 acres of thick gidgee scrub on MacFarlane, and the better country was just loaded with Bathurst and Nagoora burr. We had to get it all out before it seeded and started the cycle again, and it would have taken months to cut or chip it out with a hoe. So we decided to spray it with arsenic pentoxide, to stop it as quickly as possible. Because I wasn't

90

careful enough handling and spraying the burrs with the arsenic, it burnt off all of my fingernails, and caused some throat damage that I still have a touch of.

There was also a lot of ringbarking to start with—the tree trunks were as thick as your leg. We had to cut all around the trunk into the sapwood with an axe, and the tree would die within twelve months. The ringbarking was initially all done by hand, by us and contractors. It was pretty slow work; we might do a couple of acres a day. A few years later, in the early 1950s, contractors came in with two big D6 Caterpillar tractors, dragging between them a big steel ball on a thick chain about twenty metres or further apart. They would drive through the scrub and knock it all over. When it was dried, we'd pile it up and put a match to it. They were quite big fires.

Contractors helped us put in a couple of dams with horses that first year I was back. The tractors that came in later to clear the scrub could also dig a dam in a couple of days, rather than the months it used to take with draft horses and a scoop. That was virtually when the big draft horses went out as far as I was concerned.

Moving to Beatrice Downs from Red Knob had been a major improvement, especially for Mum, but it was an even greater improvement moving to MacFarlane. We had a telephone and a toilet in the house and a septic tank outside—it was luxury living. Mum enjoyed it; the place was only

26 mile out of the small town of Tambo, and you could go to town just about any time. The mail used to come out twice a week all year.

A shower block had been built about twenty yards from the house. There was another bathroom in the house that Mum used, but the rest of us showered outside. The shower block was right next to the big 5000-gallon (22,730-litre) soldered corrugated-iron water tank that sat about fourteen foot up on a tank stand, so we had terrific water pressure. The shower had a great big rose on it with a two-inch pipe above it—you were flat out standing under the pressure of the water that came out.

The shower room was big—six could have showered at the same time if we'd wanted to. The floor under the showers was tin, but the rest of it was six-inch pine board with great big cracks between. The walls were corrugated iron with a gap between the top of them and the roof; in winter the wind would blow in. It was dreadfully cold in winter, dear oh dear—the water used to come down the pipe, straight out of the tank, and it was freezing. There was a little chip heater that we could light up and mix its warm water in with the tank water, but the tank for the heater was only little so we didn't bother with it much.

Lach was out having a shower one afternoon, cleaning up after work, and the old tank must have been full. The solder holding the corrugated-iron tank together let go and the water burst out all down the side where the shower block was. We rushed out of the house when we heard the noise, just as a startled Lach ran out of the shower block, stark naked—he hadn't even grabbed a towel on the way out. He looked up to where the tank had been, and then around at us, and then shot straight back into the shower block to grab his towel.

We had to replace the old tank with a new one, and it was quite an effort lifting it up onto the tank stand. Arthur and I were already working on the places with Dad, but Lach, Godfrey, Ethel and Brian were still in school. However, all of us were home at this particular time. We erected these two big posts, with a pulley block on top, and we pulled the new tank up using our combined manpower. The tank was empty, of course—it would have weighed fifteen ton if it was full of water. When we got it up to the right height, we pushed it across onto the platform that was already there, and our new tank was up.

Shifting the new water tank in place at MacFarlane Downs.

*

Labour was hard to come by during the war. When we first left school, both Arthur and I were still too young to join up, but not to work. These two old men, Fred Mills and Bob Thompson, came and worked for us—well, we thought they were old at the time; they were probably in their fifties. They were returned servicemen from the First World War, and both were alcoholics. They were very reliable until they got near a full rum bottle. They were fencers and ringbarkers when they first started with us; they weren't shearers, but they could help out. Well, I sort of took them over, was their boss, but I was more a minder really. We gave them a job and a home, and they worked for us for the next ten to fifteen years.

Fencing camp at Beatrice.

We repaired twenty mile of six-foot-high dog-netting fence in one line and ten mile in another at Beatrice, and all the posts for that were cut with an axe by Fred, Bob and myself at MacFarlane Downs, which was more heavily timbered than Beatrice and Red Knob. I think we cut three thousand posts virtually in one go.

We used to travel the 300 mile between Beatrice and MacFarlane Downs a fair bit, because we provided the labour for marking the lambs, for fencing and dingo trapping, for shearing rams and stragglers, as well as for ringbarking. Arthur mainly stopped at Beatrice Downs and I used to travel with the shearing team—made up of me and two or three other men. We always shore our own lambs and the rams twice a year; we used to do nearly all our own crutching and shear any stragglers. Then at shearing time we'd get a few men in for station shearing, and myself and one or two of the brothers would take a pen beside.

The day I turned sixteen, I shore my first one hundred sheep in a day. Well, weaner lambs really, aged between six and nine months, but it was a tally I was proud of at the time. First thing the next morning the wool presser broke his jaw when the latch didn't drop in on the press; the press lever came up and hit him under the chin and smashed his jawbone. I was then promoted to wool presser, and the day after I turned sixteen, I hand-pressed sixteen bales of wool.

I was probably only about seven stone (44 kilos) wringing wet at the time, and I wasn't strong enough to finish each bale by myself. Once I had wool in the press, I couldn't push the lever all the way down, so I had to yell out to somebody to help push the last bit down; it took about thirty seconds for one of the roustabouts to come over and give me a hand. Pressing was harder than shearing when I was starting out. Now, with hydraulic presses, it's easy—a wool presser pushes the wool in, presses a button and walks away to collect more wool.

One of the hardest things about shearing a sheep back then was the number of really wrinkly sheep. They were like a concertina—fold upon fold of skin and wool, not just on their necks but all over—and were a nightmare to shear.

The Vermont breed was one of the worst things that ever happened to the wool industry. Samuel McCaughey was a real innovator in a lot of agricultural areas back then and made a lot of money. He was based all over Victoria, South Australia, New South Wales and western Queensland. In 1886 he went to America and first bought these high-priced Vermont sheep, mostly rams, and he'd bring them out in lots of a hundred. A lot of people decided to follow him, because he was so prosperous and such an innovator, but it was a catastrophe.

The Vermont was so wrinkly—they looked like a woolly brain on legs. The original thinking with the Vermont was that there would be more wool, because of those great big folds, but not really. The extra weight of the wool was all grease and lanolin not just wool; not only that, but you couldn't shear them in the wrinkles to get the wool anyway, and then of course the folds made perfect warm dark homes for blowfly maggots.

Example of Vermont sheep—Hugh Tindall Collection

With fly strike, the fly lays eggs on the skin of the sheep among the warm wool—it's best for the fly if the wool is damp. The eggs hatch into larvae in this nice warm moist environment; they feed on the sheep's skin and will eat into them, eventually poisoning the sheep and killing them. All sheep are susceptible to being struck during long wet seasons, and wool needs to be removed from damp areas when flies are about; we crutch and shear them to get air onto the skin and reduce the risk of fly strike.

Everyone followed McCaughey, breeding with the Vermont until he lost hundreds of thousands of sheep— possibly even a million—in 1902 to fly strike. After that he decided to go back to the Peppin merino bloodlines. Nowadays they breed merinos with straight bodies and necks; the rams don't even have folds on their necks, they are more or less straight, minimal wrinkles. They get just as much wool without those folds, strangely enough, because the sheep can walk around better and they're not as prone to getting wool blind, like they used to be.

There used to be an image of a ram on the early ten-cent pieces, and before that the old shilling used to have a ram on it as well, celebrating their idea of the perfect merino, with lots of folds of wool on his neck. But those big folds have gone out of fashion, same as the wrinkly Vermonts. Back when I started to shear there were still wrinkly sheep, a legacy of the Vermont breeding but you wouldn't have a Vermont now—you'd cut its throat rather than have it back.

Chapter 14

Shooting roos, dingoes and pigs

IN BLACKALL IN 1948, ten thousand roo skins a week used to go away on the train to skin dealers in Brisbane and they were sold all over the world. Just like with the wool, we would send them down to the agent and get a cheque back after they were sold. Roo skin is one of the strongest leathers of any in the world. And it's really soft. R.M. Williams use them for dress boots—roo-hide boots are the ultimate. An ordinary bootlace made out of roo skin and not even a millimetre thick is incredibly strong—you'd have to pull pretty hard to break it. And roo skin is hard wearing—you can put it on the sole of a slipper, it wears so well.

These days, a lot of people overseas object to us shooting our kangaroos. But they are a pest—one place up at Hughenden shot ten thousand roos last year and it didn't make any difference on that place at all. Roos breed all the time. The thing with roos is that they are floating populations—if there's a drought, they'll move somewhere else. Where you see the roos, that's where the best feed in the district is. They can easily get through ordinary fences, and can sometimes get through the dog-netting fences, or they get caught up in them and die.

Arthur, Hugh, Godfrey and Lach heading off roo shooting.

We mostly used guns to control the roos, dingoes and foxes, and sometimes we'd also put out strychnine baits to control the foxes and dingoes. You sprinkle the bright pink powder onto cubes of meat and set them along fence lines for the foxes and dingoes to find.

You had to be careful of your own dogs, of course. You can save a dog that's taken a bait if you're quick. You have to put a stick in their mouth so they don't bite you unintentionally when they have a fit, and then you pour salt, a handful of it, down their neck and make them vomit. Once they've brought up the bait, there's no problem. They generally have three fits. You have the best chance of saving them if you get them to vomit after the first fit. If you do it on the second fit, you'll probably save them 50 per cent of the time; but by the third one, unless there's a vet on hand, they'll most likely die.

Out on the Diamantina, you'd see them take the bait or have the first fit, and you wouldn't always have salt on you. But if you were near the house then any salt—whether fine or the coarse salt that you make corned beef with—you'd grab and use. I remember seeing Dad do it with a couple of dogs, and I did it myself when I was about fourteen. But we were always too far away to get the dog to a vet in time. It's a fairly quick death with strychnine, but with arsenic, which we didn't use much, it's a horrid lingering death.

As well as everything else, when it was wet we had to deal with pigs. In the channel country and on the Thomson you'd see them as they spread out about twenty mile from the water. I went out riding one morning when we'd had about half an inch of rain the night before, and I came across a ewe standing by herself and I knew there was something wrong. I went over and saw there were pig tracks—a pig had taken her lamb. So I followed the tracks and found the remains of another lamb. I kept following and came across another half-eaten lamb—the one pig had killed three lambs that morning.

With the rain that had fallen and on the black soil, he was easy to follow, this tremendous big boar pig, going through a mob of sheep. His tracks were just like following a crawling caterpillar. He was a big heavy pig, and he got shot pretty quickly.

We were still using horses all the time for mustering, breaking them in ourselves, and we rode them when we were running dingo, especially on Beatrice and Red Knob, so close to the barrier fence. Us four older boys all had a revolver strapped onto the pummel of the saddle. It didn't matter which horse you got on and which saddle you used because you always had a revolver there.

In that low stunted gidgee country you'd be ducking and diving following a dingo, and you needed both hands to steer. If they got a good lead on you, they'd run for miles and miles, but if you got onto a dingo within 100 yards and began cooeeing and yelling, they started squirting out the backside in panic and knock up quickly. If you didn't have a revolver, you'd have to hit it with a stick, or pull your stirrup iron off and try and hit him on the head. A dingo not being knocked up is dangerous. I never got bitten, but it was close before I was given a gun. With a revolver, as soon as the dingo pulled up, you'd just shoot and he was dead.

The policeman stationed at Stonehenge used to come out with the mailman for a look around, once or twice a year. He'd just do it to check how things were around Warbreccan and Connemara, all along the mail route. One time they pulled up at Beatrice Downs while my brothers and I were breaking in horses, and there we were—attached to all our saddles were unregistered revolvers.

He came alongside to talk to us, and saw the revolvers. He walked over to the first horse, pulled a gun out of its holster and fired it; then he put it back. He went to the next one—bang! He went through all four guns and I thought, 'Oh, we're done for the lot.' But he didn't say anything; he just walked away and said, 'Have a good day.'

You never travelled out there without a rifle in your vehicle, generally just in front of the steering wheel, or we'd put them between the seat and the back wall in clamps that came out of old army Blitze vehicles—just a little bucket to hold the butt and a small clamp. We had .303s to start with, but then later on we got high-powered .250s or .280s. Most of the rifles had telescopic sights, and we could shoot spot-on at 400 yards.

Out there, everyone carried a gun out to work every day. Every time you went out you would come across feral pigs on the river, dingoes, wild dogs and foxes; there were thousands of eaglehawks (wedge-tailed eagles). A gun was the best way to eradicate them.

Chapter 15

Buckjumpers

OF COURSE, IT wasn't all work. As long as everything was done, I could still fit in a bit of socialising. At MacFarlane I used to go into Tambo to play football, cricket and tennis and chase the girls. But I never had any luck with the girls.

When I was about seventeen, I went over to the larger town of Blackall, forty eight mile from MacFarlane one day to get some work done on a Chev ute—its 1000-mile check—and I knew this bloke Sam Fuller was organising a buckjump show that night, so I thought I'd stay and watch it.

There was a vacant allotment right next to the post office, and Sam and some of the jackaroos from around the area had made a makeshift ring there. They put in these ten-foot-high posts and tied ropes around them for a fence. They got buckjumping horses from around the district and brought them into town—the horses were all broken in, but they could really buck. There was no chute or anything like that, just a ring with a gate. They'd lead in a horse one at a time, put the saddle on and invite somebody to come in and ride it. If you could ride it for the designated time it was about two pound prize money, a small fortune.

There was a lovely girl working at Smiths Garage where I took the Chev, and I was always trying to get her to go out with me and she had always said no. Anyway, while I was there I asked her to the buckjump show that night and she agreed. I couldn't believe it. I was over the moon.

It was a bitterly cold night and this girl and I were sitting right up the back of the raised seating set up around the ring, quite high, sitting close together trying to stay warm as we watched the buckjumping. They led the last horse out—Black Mamba was its name—and they couldn't get anyone to ride it. They offered five pound, then ten pound to anybody who was game and could stay on this horse. Then they called out, 'Hugh Tindall, you come down here—you've got a bit of a rep.' But I refused—I wasn't going to leave this girl I was snuggled up to. Eventually I said, 'I haven't got any boots,' and a pair of boots came flying up at me. And then I said, 'I haven't any spurs,' so a pair of spurs came flying up. Not feeling like I had much choice, I put them on and made my way down into the makeshift ring. I should have known better.

Black Mamba just stood there as I got on, and she still stood there with me sitting on top. I thought, 'This is going to be easy!' The bloke who had been holding her while I got on then walked behind her and hit her on the rump with a spare bridle he was holding. She took off, bucking around the ring. I reckon she went three times around the ring before I knew it. I thought, 'Oh golly, I really am going to ride this horse'—the ten pounds was as good as mine.

We were going around the ring for the fourth time, and as we went past this girl, I held my hat up to her and, being smart, gave her a 'cooee'. The next thing I knew I was hanging over the top rope, about eight foot off the ground like a wet towel.

I got down, so embarrassed. This bloke said, 'Well done, Hughie—you rode her a lot longer than anyone else has ever ridden her. But not enough for the ten pounds.' And I didn't mind, because I was just thinking, 'I'll be right with this girl now.' So I had a bit of a grin; I threw the boots and spurs back to their owner, and went to where this girl had been sitting. But she'd gone. So I missed out on even shaking hands at the gate, or a peck on the cheek.

We used to catch and ride brumbies running out on the Vergemont, so I was breaking in horses all the time. We'd put our mares out there and bring them back in foal to the brumby stallions, and the resulting foals were the best horses of the lot. They were a lot tougher than the thoroughbreds, which weren't much good in that rough country—it was too hard for them.

I never went around with rodeos; they weren't a big

thing then anyway. But people would bring horses to me that used to buck a bit. I generally got them to bring out their horses after it had rained. Then I'd lead them off from another horse about a mile into a claypan where there was a bluebush swamp that after rain would have about a foot of water in it with deep mud. I'd ride a quiet horse down and have a saddle on the problem one; then, when we got into the middle of the swamp, I'd transfer over—they couldn't buck in the water. I then rode the horse around and it seemed to take the buck out of them. I never told anybody at the time that this was what I was doing. So I ended up with a reputation for taking the buck out of these horses— and I don't even like horses!

I remember one horse I broke in, a big strong horse; he'd let you get on, but as soon as you went to move off, even if you'd turned him out for a week or been riding him every day, he would start up bucking. He was like a great big rocking horse—tremendous. His name was Pivot and he was really spectacular, but the fact was anyone could have ridden him—you just sat there while he bucked backwards and forwards a few times, and then he moved off and did a day's work. People would see me on him, up in the air, so I got an even bigger reputation for riding bucking horses. But I didn't deserve it at all.

Back then there were dances every weekend at the local halls in all the towns, big and small. Local musicians supplied the music and everyone brought their own food and drink. At Tambo there'd be a dance every Saturday night at the little tin hall, which was too small for the numbers that came—there were probably eighty to a hundred people each time. All ages would go, from kids up. For quite a few years I was the master of ceremonies at our local Tambo hall. There was no PA system—just a piano, maybe drums, sometimes a sax, depending on which locals played on the night. Most women, and a lot of men, could play the piano then, and everyone knew the songs.

The big social week in Longreach was the first week in May—May week, we called it. You had the Catholic debutantes' ball, the Church of England deb ball, the Race Club ball, the Annual Show ball—four balls one after another, and then a big dance at the end. One year I partnered a girl to both deb balls. Then you had the ram sales one day, the races over two days, and the show ran over another two days. We just buggered around the other days of the week.

Everyone could dance back then—we used to do the Gypsy Tap, the Pride of Erin and the waltz. No one taught us to dance as kids; we just went to dances and joined in. You'd be knee high and your mother would pick you up and waltz around the room with you. Most of the men and boys could dance, and they taught the younger girls.

One of our neighbours at Tambo was Jim Miller. He and Dad were both twelve years older than their wives and coincidentally they both married their wives on the same weekend, one in New South Wales and the other in Queensland. Then they had four boys each, then one girl, then another boy. The Millers' house was a big old Queenslander on high blocks in the town. We'd often visit and do things together, and they'd come out to our house; we'd go shooting, play tennis, all the things kids do. We all grew up together. Their son Sid and I were about the same age and we were great mates.

Mrs Miller was a good pianist, and if there was nothing else on in the area, she'd get on the piano and we'd be dancing and singing on the verandah. But there weren't enough girls for us teenage boys to dance with. There were three or four other families who would join us—the Bassingtons had twelve kids, ten of which were boys. There must have been something in the water.

One time Mrs Miller reckoned she'd get a couple of older girls to come along and dance with us. I was doing my best, trying to get friendly with one of these girls, but not getting anywhere. Sid was back that weekend from studying at university, where he was training to be a vet, and he had been going out with girls and doing things that we only dreamed of. For us, going out with a girl meant shaking hands at the gate at the end of the night, that sort of business. With all his experience Sid couldn't believe he wasn't getting any results with these two girls, but we found out years after that the girls Mrs Miller had invited were both lesbians. Sid often said his mum was a very shrewd woman.

Chapter 16

Bob and Fred

WHEN ARTHUR TURNED eighteen in 1943 he wanted to join the army. But because all the other young men from the bush had already gone, he, myself and several others on the land who turned eighteen towards the end of the Second World War were told to stay and work. The army registered us but told us to go home and we'd be called up if needed. I was told point blank to go home and look after my sheep!

It was a bit tough. There was some finger pointing around the town, with some people thinking we were shirking our responsibilities, and after the war one neighbour all but told us we were cowards. There was no point trying to explain to him, he didn't want to listen.

Our First World War veterans, Fred and Bob, were good workers but, after about a month of working they'd get crabby. You knew what was wrong, and if we were going into town, they'd jump in. We'd drop them off at the pub and tell them we'd pick them up in a couple of days or however long we were going to be.

They'd spend all of their money at the pub, poor ole fellas. They would be joined there by a pack of 'dawnies', which is what we called the alcoholic no-hopers who would still be up drinking at dawn. The dawnies would shout Bob and Fred their first beer, but then they'd bludge off our fellows for the rest of the time. Our pair were honest old blokes, hard-working and very reliable when they were sober, but you could never rely on them after they'd had grog. They were real alcoholics, they didn't know anything else.

When we went to pick them up, they'd be camped down near the woodshed at the back of the hotel—everyone had a woodshed then. They'd be camped out without swags or anything, around a small fire, drunk. So we'd buy a bottle of rum, making sure they didn't have any before we left, and take them back home.

Back at MacFarlane, we'd give them each a small tot of rum most afternoons or just before sundown, and they looked forward to it. They wouldn't come into our house yard, but they'd be walking up and down the fence, clearing their throats, and Lach and I would be sitting on the verandah pretending we hadn't noticed, and then one of us would say, 'Oh! Rum time,' and they'd be straight in through the gate.

They were great old fellows. Bob was a real gentleman, always polite. You'd go out fencing in the morning at sunrise with old Fred and before we left he'd put a leg of mutton or something in the camp oven. We'd come back just before dark and it would be cooked to perfection.

Godfrey and Lach eventually left school and there were three of us boys at Tambo, Arthur at Beatrice, and then the sister came home and she used to cook and help Mum look after all of us. We used to take it in turns making breakfast—porridge, usually followed by lots of protein (mutton chops, steak, eggs and mince)—but Mum and then Ethel did all the other cooking. There was plenty of that.

At Tambo, Mum got her first Aga. Now, they were really good stoves, but when you poured dusty coke into them in the morning, you could get a bit of wind come up and the coke dust would blow everywhere. You had to be very careful, or you had to sweep your kitchen and clean your furniture afterwards.

When Bob died in the mid 1950's, he left his money to Ethel. Ethel got a real shock. She used to feed him and look after him—she was the main cook at MacFarlane Downs after she came home from school—but it was a real surprise. Fred passed away a few years before Bob. They were both survivors of mustard gas attacks in the First World War and had come back alcoholics and heavy smokers. They spent their last days peacefully with us at MacFarlane.

Chapter 17

Tindall and Sons

IN 1946 OUR neighbour at Beatrice Downs, Bill Springer, decided he wanted to get out and sell his place, Thurles Park. Dad went to the bank and stood guarantor for Arthur, myself, Lach and Godfrey, and so us four older boys became landowners.

This started us off and we formed a partnership, Tindall and Sons. Thurles was 36,000 acres, and when it was joined with Beatrice, right next door, we ended up with 70,000-odd acres on one aggregation, completely enclosed by a six-foot dingo-proof fence, which upgraded ourselves after purchasing Thurles. It was a bit harder and rougher country than Beatrice, and it didn't have much on it—a tin hut and a good shearing shed, and that was about it. We knew we just had to work to build it up and really make something out of it. So all the fencing and huts and water and so on we did ourselves. It didn't cost us anything much, other than a lot of sweat. We built it up from being really rundown to really good in a few years.

Thurles had one major asset in that it had a bore, not just dams. If you get a big drought the waterholes are not going to carry you through. Out there, a dam could evaporate by ten foot in a year; generally dams were put down at twenty-odd foot deep, so they could possibly last you two years without rain, but no longer

What sort of bore flow you get and how deep the water is below the ground depends on where you are in the Artesian Basin. Up around the Aramac Basin, north-east of Longreach, the Basin is within 100 foot below the surface, which means a really strong flow, but if you go out to the triangle formed by Longreach, Winton and Hughenden, where there is a fault in the land, you might need to go down 2000 feet to reach water. If you put in a second bore within a mile of that, then it might be 5000 feet before you get to the basin. That's a lot of steel casing to line to that depth, but you have to have reliable water.

The bore on Thurles was really reliable; it was about 2500 feet deep with good water at 1000 feet.

When the Second World War ended, there was a surplus of army vehicles; because of the need for transport in the bush, special consideration was given to allow farmers to purchase them ahead of others. The vehicles—jeeps, Blitz trucks, motorbikes and even small tanks—were relatively cheap and tough, and made ideal bush vehicles. They were put up for public auction on an 'as is' basis and with payment required in cash on the day. Being the mechanically minded member of the family, I left for a trip to Sydney in 1946, in an aeroplane, to have a look at what was on offer. After that, I flew down each year for the next four or five years in a row to buy a surplus vehicle, and each time I would drive it back up.

For the start of the trip I would get someone to drive me from Tambo to Charleville early in the morning. There I got into a de Havilland Dragon Rapide, which could seat about seven passengers—it was the same plane the Royal Flying Doctor was using at the time. Butler Airways owned the plane and it went for at least ten years up there I reckon. We flew in stages, picking up and letting off passengers as we went: from Charleville to Cunnamulla, Bourke, Nyngan, Coonamble and then on to Sydney. By the time we got to Sydney the streetlights would be on, and we'd have left Charleville at daylight or just before. Seeing all those lights as we came in over the Sydney suburbs into Mascot was really something for a boy from Central Queensland. They seemed to go on forever.

While I was there I would go to see the merino sheep at the Royal Easter Show. It was a big deal; all the big-name studs—Boonoke, Haddon Rig, Uadry and Merryville—and all the owners and managers would be there. I used to try to get in with the jackaroos—they were more likely to talk to a bloke from Central Queensland than the stud owners or managers were.

At that stage we were only getting sixteen pence a pound for our wool but it was still a valued commodity.

Bought in 1946, ex-army 1942 Harley Davidson motorbike that I rode from Sydney to Tambo and had for many years.

On my first trip to Sydney, I bought myself a brand-new Harley Davidson; I pulled it out of its box, put it together and headed back up to Queensland. The Harley sure was an improvement on the old rubber-belt-driven 1918 Douglas. It came complete with ammunition boxes and a rifle scabbard, an attachment to insert a rifle into.

In subsequent years I went down and bought an ex-army jeep, a Dodge Blitz weapon carrier and an Austin three-ton truck, driving them home each time after staying with relatives of Mum's for a few days. One time I loaded up my aunt and uncle, various cousins and their friends on the back of the troop carrier and we went picnicking in the Royal National Park south of Sydney and had a great day.

There were no seatbelts, just everyone in the back—couldn't do that now.

It must have been in the second year that I went down, 1947, that we got lost flying in a dust storm. We couldn't see a thing, and in a plane it's very easy to become disorientated if you can't see a horizon. The pilot brought us down pretty low but still couldn't see much. He knew we were roughly somewhere between Nyngan and Coonamble in the Macquarie marshes and he decided to put us down. An airstrip on someone's property was unheard of back then, so he just told us to look for anywhere flat he could possibly land. As we flew over this area, I yelled out, 'Look there, a claypan! We're going over a claypan!' The pilot circled back, and we came in to land.

As we approached the end of the claypan, going slow, one wheel went into a small gully and knocked the hydraulic line out at the bottom of the wheel. I was seated beside the door, and when we hit the gully we stopped and I sort of fell out the door when I was bounced onto it and landed behind the wing—there were no passenger seatbelts in planes then. I looked over and saw there was an oil leak. I was right close to it, so I reached up and put my finger over the hose. I knew enough about hydraulics to put a stop to the flow and hopefully maintain some oil. When the pilot jumped out, he saw me stopping up the end of the loose hydraulic hose, so he got a pair of pliers from the plane. There was a fence a couple of hundred yards away and we used the pliers to cut a length of wire off it, and

I tied the hose back to the connection with a Cobb & Co knot and stopped the leak.

The people who owned the place had seen us land, and they came down in an old truck and took us back to their place for the night. The next morning we all got back in the plane and flew off to Coonamble and then Sydney, with a piece of wire still holding the hydraulic line in place. Once I told this story to an airline pilot I met who flies big jets all around the world, and he wouldn't believe me, but it's true—we flew on to Sydney with nothing but a piece of wire holding a broken hydraulic connection.

Chapter 18

Working with sheep

ONE OF THE main jobs we had to do on all our places was lamb marking—docking their tails, castrating the ram lambs and earmarking. Lach and I could mark six lambs a minute for, say, two hours non-stop.

We used Shannon cradles, which were invented by a bloke called Shannon from out between Ilfracombe and Longreach. You placed the lambs in the cradles on their back, their tail towards you. You marked them, then tipped the cradle and let them onto the ground to go find their mums after you finished each one. I used to make the cradles and modify them. I started by making ten cradles in a line but found that was too hard to handle, so I brought them back to six or four and then we could join them up together, in sets of two or three, to get a long line.

I was constantly improving the design. At first we just had a corn bag at the base of the cradle for the lambs to slide down when released, but I found that when you tipped them out they weren't landing on their feet. So I put tin slides at the base of each cradle, and put cuts in the bottom of the tin to hook onto their wool and tip them up when they slid down. Then they landed on their feet.

Back then ordinary people constantly invented and improved farm gear, because they could see how something could be made a little better with modifications. Out in some of that backcountry it was hard to get shearers, and some places weren't big enough for sheds, so a new kind of shearing machine was invented. They used to call it the 'husband-and-wife unit'. The wife hand-turned a big or small wheel—like a bike wheel with a handle on it—which was geared down to provide the energy for the handpiece, so the husband could shear the sheep. There must have been some wives out there with big arm muscles, as it was quite hard monotonous work constantly turning the wheel, doing the work of the modern overhead gear used today. The units were only used on smaller places, those with twenty to two hundred sheep, and were quite ingenious.

Another clever innovation was developed to stop rams damaging each other. Sometimes rams fight a lot, especially if they're not doing much work. When rams want to fight, they look at one another, then put their head down before they charge. So someone came up with the idea of putting a leather blind on them, tied over their horns with two little straps; when the ram put its head down, the blind fell over its eyes so it could only see down and to the side, not straight ahead; because it couldn't see the other ram, it wouldn't be able to fight. There were a lot of very clever innovations in the bush—out of necessity, I suppose.

Tindall and Sons now shore about twenty-five thousand sheep on the four places—MacFarlane Downs, Beatrice, Thurles Park and Red Knob. Red Knob was used more as a drought-relief block; also, if we had a bit of overstock, we could put some there for a few months.

We never had anyone living permanently at Red Knob while we had sheep there. Red Knob had to be constantly checked for dingoes by one of us. I rode out one time with a packhorse, intending to be away for a week. Trouble started when I saw there were two dingoes inside the fence; I couldn't go home till they were both caught, but they were being elusive. At the end of two weeks I had only half a tin of jam left and enough flour for a couple of small dampers— that was all. I would mix up some flour and water, flatten it to about half an inch thick and throw it into the hot coals; it was OK if eaten hot, otherwise it would get hard as a stone. There was plenty of rock salt in the sheep troughs, which improved the taste of the flock pigeon or galah stew that I made at night. As it happened, I found the last dingo just after I'd used the absolute last bit of flour I had with me.

Lach, Godfrey and I organised the shearing and crutching on all the blocks, and often worked away in the shearing teams. Over the years, shearers' strikes came and went, for various reasons. There was a strike in late 1947, but it wasn't too bad. Up till then the shearers had to work four hours on a Saturday morning, which meant they were working a forty-four-hour week; they were striking to bring the hours down to a forty-hour week, plus they wanted an early cut-out (finish) on the Friday. In the end, Saturday-morning shearing was abolished, which brought shearing in line with the forty-hour week, but the shearers still wanted to knock off half an hour to an hour earlier on Friday afternoon as well.

Well, it was a bit embarrassing as far as I was concerned. I was shearing at our different places with them and, because I was also often shearing my own sheep, I kept on shearing until half past five on a Friday, the usual knock-off time, to work a forty-hour week; the other blokes would just be standing there looking at me. My argument was that the award hadn't actually been changed, and the time had to be on the clock so I kept shearing.

But then on some Friday mornings, I'd go up to the shed and the clock would be wound forward an hour; instead of starting at seven thirty, as it stated on the clock, we were actually starting at 6.30 a.m. Wristwatches weren't common then, so if the clock stated it was seven thirty, you could start an hour early and knock off an hour early. And that's how they got around it.

Eventually, of course, we got to where we are now. The young shearers these days are pretty good and they're making good money; sometimes they want to get away early so they start earlier. Back then, however, the clock was what dictated start-up and knock-off times, and the other shearers weren't allowed to leave the shed while I was still shearing because of the award. But then of course some of them would have to go to the toilet half an hour before knock-off, so all of them would go to the toilet, and I'd be left shearing by myself or with a couple of my brothers. The shearers never said anything; they knew what the union award stated.

Chapter 19

The big flood

IN 1950 IT rained—really rained. I think there was 44 inches out at Beatrice, Red Knob and Thurles that year (the average for Longreach was about sixteen or eighteen inches; at Beatrice it was fourteen). That rainfall figure in 1950 might have been beaten a couple of times since—in the late 1970s, say—but that was the wettest year we'd seen up till then. All over western New South, Queensland and the Northern Territory, the floodwaters stayed up for the longest time ever.

Floods were nothing new to anyone living out there. As I've already described, most wet seasons the channels would fill and you'd get flooded in. The Thomson River could be six mile wide in January or February some years, but it was usually only a couple of feet deep—just an inconvenience really. But the big floods were something else. From January 1950 to June 1951, we had flood after flood all over the state, with unseasonal rain constantly topping up already swollen rivers and creeks.

We had bought five thousand ewes from up the river at Bimerah, not far past Stonehenge, but because it kept raining and the river rose, we couldn't go and get them. So they were left there for probably another six weeks before we could shift them. Permanent bridges had been built in the late 1940s, finally replacing the old suspension bridge and rowboat, but in big floods the bridges were still cut off. When the river went down enough, we managed to get the sheep to walk across them; without those permanent bridges, we'd have had to wait for weeks longer.

Fred helping cross the ewes from Bimerah at the crossing on the bridge that replaced the old suspension bridge.

Because of the delay, the ewes started lambing along the way—just about when we got to Stonehenge. So I put a crate on the back of the one-ton utility and I had a couple of hundred lambs in there as we slowly walked the ewes to Beatrice. I'd drive the lambs to where we were going to camp at lunchtime, so they could find their mums when they arrived, and mother up and get a suck of milk. Sometimes I'd have to pick them up again, if they weren't strong enough to walk with their mum to the next stop. We repeated the slow trek until we made it home, and thankfully before the river came up again.

In 1950, when it rained through winter, shearing teams were trapped by floodwater all over the place, and sheep owners were getting desperate to get the wool off their sheep. Those shearers caught in the unseasonal floods might not get to us for three months—they had to stop in the shearers' quarters wherever they were until the water went down. When the floods allowed, the contractors moved the shearers around on a big truck. Often they'd have a portable engine to run the overhead gear in the small cocky sheds.

I was at Tambo when I heard from Arthur that he was having trouble out at Beatrice with fly strike in the long wool as shearing had been delayed for so long. The floodwaters were still up, but we had to go over there and shear the sheep or we'd start to lose them. He went out to muster the sheep closer to the shed, and Lach, Godfrey, Bill, Fred and I loaded up the big Dodge Blitz truck with everything we thought we'd need for a few weeks away.

The Thomson was still in full flood and the roads from Longreach to Beatrice were impassable, so we decided to drive from Tambo to Longreach by road and see if we could make our way down the river road in the truck. It took us two days to go 100 mile, trying to follow the river road in the Blitz, and using a 44-gallon drum plus another 60 gallons of fuel; we slowly ploughed through the mud and swollen creeks, trying not to get bogged.

We finally arrived at Stonehenge. Both new bridges over the channels were submerged, so I swam out and collected the council's big flat-bottomed steel boat. We loaded as much as we could into it and headed out across the six mile of river to where Arthur would be waiting for us on the other side. We had enough gear and supplies to fill the boat twice, so we'd have to make two trips. As we headed out for the first journey we were so laden that the rim of the boat was only just sitting above the water. Earlier, the council boatman had had trouble with the new outboard; while trying to fix it, he'd dropped the motor in about twenty foot of water and couldn't retrieve it. So there was nothing for it but to row across. We had to row six mile one way, come back six mile, and then go six mile back again that night.

The five of us climbed into the boat and headed off. We made our way through the maze of submerged bushes and shallow sections. I said to Bob and Fred, 'One of you blokes has got to row over to start with,' but nearly halfway across Bob gets an oar caught in a partially submerged lignum bush and nearly turns us all over, three or four miles from land. I thought, 'Righto, I'm going to row—because I'm not going to swim.' We got over there, fully loaded, with only a couple of boards for us all to sit on among the supplies. After we unloaded the first lot I still felt fresh and said to the others that I'd go back and get the second load while everyone else set up camp for the night. I rowed back across that afternoon, and loaded up the boat for the second trip.

Setting off to row across the flooded Thomson River.

It was just on dark when I started to row back. There was no moon up at that stage, and it was incredible—the stars just lit up the water around me and I could make out the dark shapes of the submerged trees and most of the bushes as I slowly rowed my way back. The stars out there are different altogether, the night sky so clear the stars seem brighter, and their reflection on the water was providing some light, but I still couldn't see where on the other bank I needed to head to. I knew I'd be rowing due west on the way back, I also knew where the Southern Cross was in the night sky, but I could be 200 mile down the river and the Southern Cross would still look like it was in the same place.

There was a hill on Arthur's side of the channel and I told them before I left, 'You blokes need to have a fire going on that rise if I'm not back before midnight.' Every so often I'd glance back over my shoulder and look for the fire to row towards, and when they finally lit it, just before midnight, I was very relieved. I corrected my course and steadily made it to the other side. I had to constantly check my direction by looking over my shoulder, but at least I felt confident which direction I was going in. It really was too far for just one person in the dark—I should have taken someone else back across the river with me to share the rowing, but I just thought I was bulletproof.

I finally arrived just before daybreak and Arthur was there with the others, his truck loaded with the supplies we'd brought over on the first trip. We loaded the rest of the supplies I'd brought over and all headed off. We still had another 40 mile to go to the shed, and Arthur had the sheep waiting.

By the time we got to the shed, I was pretty tired. I always used to shear at number one stand because that meant

I could do the counting out of shorn sheep and the grinding of combs and cutters. But on that day I noticed that every time I bent over, I had shooting pains across my backside. I pulled down my pants and there were two enormous red sores, one on each cheek. Sitting on the hard planks and all the rowing back and forth over the river had caused two big painful blisters, which had since burst with the shearing.

It was very painful, and everybody had a good laugh. I realised I wasn't going to be able to bend over and shear like that, so I cut the backside out of my pants, leaving two flaps hanging down like little curtains. It was funny for everyone else, until I started shearing again; then one of my brothers said, 'Hugh, I can't stand it—every time I look up, there's two big red eyes staring back at me.' So they made me shift down the end to number six stand for the rest of shearing, where no one had to look at my backside.

Chapter 20

Fire, plague and disease

ALMOST IMMEDIATELY AFTER big rains, the blood-sucking insects would swarm and literally suck the life out of you if you were anywhere near the water. After floods I've seen sand flies in such big numbers that they killed more kangaroos than the shooters ever did. The kangaroos' eyes would bung up from bites and get infected, and they would go blind. Then they couldn't get around or eat. Even the dingoes would try to only get about in the dark, when the sand flies weren't so active. They'd get in a cave or in under bushes until nightfall, before venturing out to hunt the easy pickings of blind animals.

When the sand flies were at their worst, all the hair would come off the kangaroos' ears, and it would often fall out along their backs as well. It was no good shooting the kangaroos for their skins when they were like that—when you went to skin them, there would be a massive blob of congealed blood lying in a layer underneath, and the skin would tear apart when you went to pull it from the carcass. The skins were unusable.

After big floods there'd be a huge body of grass, and we had to watch out for fires. We had a pretty big bushfire on MacFarlane Downs after the grass dried out in 1951, and in that open country it just took off. The fire was started by lightning. It was a dry storm, no rain in it at all—you'd see the lightning hit the ground, and five minutes later you'd see smoke go up. I watched the storm and there were about six strikes one after another, all within three mile, and each strike started a fire.

By the time we got down to the fires, they had all joined up into one fire front. We raced out there with the vehicles and only basic firefighting gear; eventually we got on top of it, but we lost sheep, probably a thousand, and even the kangaroos couldn't get away in time. We shot a few hundred sheep and kangaroos after we put out the fire; you can't leave them with bad burns—the only way to help them out is to shoot them.

The large amounts of grass after a big wet season also brought out the mice and rats. They can breed up quick when there is plenty of feed. In 1950 we had an almighty rat plague. The first sign of them was when you were travelling at night and you'd see them on the edges of the road or scurrying across in front of you as you drove along. Before then, I remember rat plagues in the 1930s, then in the 1940s—there was probably one every ten to fifteen years.

Mice plagues happened as well, but not usually at the same time as the rats kept the mice numbers down. Mice just get into everything. It would get so bad that they'd get into your swag with you when you were out droving, which could be a bit disconcerting.

One weekend, Lachlan, Godfrey and I had been fixing flood-damaged fences. As usual, we knocked off Saturday lunchtime and shot through to Stonehenge, Jundah or Windorah for a dance. We wouldn't get home till just about sunrise on Monday morning—it was a long way to travel each way, and we often took Fred and Bob into the pub on Saturday and picked them up on the Sunday night when we were travelling back.

We were travelling back late this Sunday night, and at about two in the morning I got tired. We'd picked up the two old fellas, Bill and Fred, from the pub on the way out of town and we were coming down from Longreach on the road to Stonehenge, down the river. I'd seen plenty of rats around and knew they were everywhere, so I pulled onto this great big claypan to camp for the rest of the night. The big claypans often run parallel with creeks and rivers and are absolutely dead flat and white—at night they look like snow. The rats don't like going out onto them at night, because the owls will see them and pick them off. So I thought it would be a good place to camp for a couple of hours until we were ready to set off again.

Some people may not know that bushmen often sleep, especially when camping, in the same clothes they wear for work. They take off their hat and crush down the crown, and put on it their pipe and tobacco, their false teeth, their watch and whatever they happen to have on them. On that night we were just about asleep and old Bob yelled out, 'The rat's got me teeth, the rat's got me teeth!' And here was a big buck rat with Bob's false top teeth. The rat was scurrying around trying to get away, to hide under something, anything, and it was holding the teeth in its mouth in such a way that, in the moonlight, it looked like it had a great big shiny white grin as it ran around us in panic.

Godfrey and I were chasing it, and Godfrey gave this rat an almighty kick and knocked it over. We pounced on the stunned rat and Godfrey grabbed the teeth out of the rat's mouth and held them out. 'Here you go, Bob,' he said. Bob came over and said, 'Oh, thanks,' and popped them straight into his own mouth without a thought.

After the big floods in 1950, most people lost fences. During the early 1900s, they had put in what they called a dingo barrier fence, all the way from Hughenden right down to South Australia. It was a six-foot dog-netting fence, and in the 1920s and 1930s, after the First World War, boundary riders, often returned servicemen, were hired to patrol and repair it.

The boundary riders were positioned roughly every twenty mile along the fence, depending on water availability, and they were responsible for the upkeep of their section. A bloke would base himself in the middle, and go ten mile one way and ten mile the other. They rode the boundaries all the time, generally on horseback, or horse and buggy. Their job was purely to repair and maintain the fence. The pigs, roos and emus created problems by pushing under or through it; the dingoes generally tried to dig underneath, but the boundary riders maintained what they called foot netting, which was sunk down into the ground to stop the dingoes digging under. The yellowy shale in some parts could rot the galvanised netting, so some of the stuff in the ground would weaken and the dingoes could get in anywhere then. But it was very effective for forty to fifty years, until the fence posts started to get rotten, and then the 1950 flood took some sections out.

There was a boundary rider on the end of Red Knob in the early 1930s, Mr Hurkett. He and his wife Mary and their two boys, Norman and Harry, lived on the fence line. I remember them living out there in this old tin hut, but Mr Hurkett died when I was still very young, and Mrs Hurkett and the boys left not long after. I never met their dad—well, I saw him when I was a little kid, but I never spoke with him. Mr Hurkett was the last boundary rider I knew of on our section of fence; there could have been someone after that, but I don't know.

After her husband died, Mrs Hurkett went into Longreach with the boys, and for many years she cooked for the policeman in the old police station there. I don't think she was running a boarding house, but because Dad and Mum knew her, we sometimes bunked in their cottage when we visited. After she finished her job cooking for the policeman, she used to come out when I was looking after myself at Red Knob after the war. I don't know if it was Dad or Mum who organised it, but by golly I used to be glad when this old lady would get off the mail truck, come in and set about baking. She used to cook lamingtons and cakes and was a good old cook, and I loved it after looking after myself.

Mrs Hurkett feeding poddy lambs at Red Knob.

From 1944 through to 1950, I'd go out to Red Knob at different times to look after the place. In 1949 Arthur got married to a lovely girl from Sydney called Eva, and after that I used to mostly stop with them at Beatrice. Somebody had to be out at Red Knob every so often, chasing dingoes, trapping them—that was the main job, even more so after the fence went in 1950 and wasn't replaced. There was hundreds of mile of fences washed away in the channel country, and then the dingoes really started coming in. It was almost a full-time job keeping their numbers down and protecting the sheep. The problem was when some bloke twenty mile away didn't have sheep and didn't give a damn. We felt we were protecting the whole of Queensland from dingoes—we were trying to protect ourselves, and by doing that we were protecting everyone else.

There was still a lot of sheep around Hughenden and Longreach in the 1950s, but there was a gradual decrease from about 1956 on. Slowly the cattle moved in, largely because of the dingo problem.

In 1950, after the floods subsided, our sheep suddenly got ill. Initially we didn't know why. The sheep were scratching more than usual and there was wool rubbed off on fences. It turned out the problem was lice. After the big flood, people had brought sheep in from New South and they'd brought lice into the area. We'd never had lice out there until then; I didn't know what they were. Lousy sheep can lose condition from the irritation, and they rub so much that their wool gets matted, so the shearers hate shearing them.

We all had to put in Buzacott or Lister spray dips to treat the lice. Most of us had the Buzacott. These were big round pens that looked a bit like a corrugated-iron water tank from the outside; they're about ten foot across and the spray comes in underneath and over the top. You'd dip a penful of sheep at a time. You could get rid of lice completely, except if the next-door neighbour didn't treat and a lousy sheep got through a fence into your place. Then you'd have to treat everything again. So we used to put stray sheep through the Buzacott as a matter of course. Let's face it, your next-door neighbours can be nice people, but generally some of them will put things off until tomorrow. So if I ever saw one of their sheep among ours, I'd generally spray the whole mob again.

Lice weren't much of a problem north of Longreach, but when they were brought up from the south to areas around us, they more or less stayed. Down around Tambo they also had stomach worms, but there were no worms up in the north and west—it was too dry. Here's the thing about worms in the dry country: as long as you haven't got a bore drain where the worm eggs could survive, you can put all your sheep in a paddock and then after ten days shift them into a 'clean' paddock, one that hasn't had sheep in it for a while. If you do that across two or three paddocks, you'll generally get rid of the worms. We never had any footrot or liver fluke—wouldn't know what it looked like. All we had was blowflies.

There was another thing we had out in the west that was a bit unique to the area—fluoride poisoning. When kids from out around Julia Creek and Richmond go down to the city for school and have their teeth checked up, the dentist will know as soon as they open their mouth if they are from those areas—there is not a single cavity. Out in those places, one or two parts per million of fluoride is found naturally in the bore water they're drinking, and they never got holes in their teeth. But some of the bores around Blackall have too much fluoride. I've seen young stud rams from Terrick Terrick that are broken-mouthed and with sharp pointy teeth, a telltale sign of too much fluoride.

Once I had three thousand weaned wether lambs in a paddock with a bore that was pumping a lot of water down a bore drain for about a mile into a big flat lagoon. Every so often we would 'delve' all the bore drains, including this one, to clear them. They would get choked up with both grass and the sheep walking through them, plugging them up, so you wanted to delve them out once a month in the summertime and once or twice in winter. The drain was generally a great long trough; when you got that built-up mud out, it flowed better. Originally, bullocks were used to pull delving ploughs along the bore drains, then horses were used, and later tractors of course. The plough has a point on it and arms on either side, so you can raise or lower it to any depth.

Anyhow, there were three thousand weaners in this paddock, supposedly putting on weight, but instead they were getting poor. I couldn't figure out why. I was following them one day and one just fell over in front of me. I ran over to him to try and save him, and I opened his mouth and worked it out straight away. His teeth were all falling out, pointy and rotten, and he couldn't eat. It was fluoride poisoning.

When the wind whipped up, over a period of time the water would evaporate, leaving large concentrated amounts of fluoride in the bore drain and around its edges.

So I moved them out of the paddock and flushed the bore drain. We eventually replaced open drains with poly pipe and troughs and that meant no more delving and reduced evaporation. There are a lot of things will kill a sheep, and over time I've probably seen most of them.

Chapter 21

The wool boom

THE PRICE OF wool had been held down during the Second World War by an agreement between the Australian, New Zealand and South African governments and England for the war effort, known as the Joint Organisation (JO). This was so the war effort always had cheap wool for their uniforms. After the war the price rose a little, because they could get transport with the boats running again, and the JO was eventually disbanded.

In 1950, something occurred that I think was one of the worst things that ever happened to the wool industry, worse than any disease—the start of the Korean War. The Americans demanded wool for their troops' uniforms, because of the bitter Korean winter; they tried to enter into something similar to the old JO agreement, but it didn't eventuate. So, without any agreement in place, the wool sold on the free market, and the price went up to a pound for a pound (454 grams). One pound Australian for a pound of wool.

Just imagine, the price of wool went from sixteen pence to 240 pence per pound of wool. It was unbelievable. I wasn't very politically aware about the Korean War, but I was certainly aware of what it was doing to the price of wool. All of Australia was 'riding on the sheep's back'.

The really big prices—240 pence or more per pound—probably lasted only two months. We certainly never got any of it; we shore at the wrong time of year, and shearing had also been held up by the floods. The price didn't go right back down to sixteen pence, but it went back to nearly halfway between—just over 144 pence per pound of wool. In today's money, the grower would get around the equivalent of forty dollars a kilo (today they get an average of four to five dollars per kilo).

It was a good time to be in the wool industry—for us, and for all of Australia. But I still maintain that the 1950 boom was the worst thing that ever happened to the wool industry. Everyone hopped on the gravy train and wanted to spend up big. Some people had never had so much money before in their lives; they went into town and had great parties and went to the Gold Coast and Brisbane, buying racehorses and having an absolute ball. It was a bad reflection on all the graziers, flashing their money around. What happened next was that everybody seemed to think that all the graziers got top dollar for their wool. They didn't—most only got half of that, although that was still a lot. But because of the increase in the amount of money in the bush, supplies of agricultural equipment dwindled and you couldn't buy netting, piping for water, windmills, trucks or tractors. You couldn't even buy a car—you had to put your name down for probably six months to buy a new Holden.

For us, the Tindall boys, the wool boom helped us pay off our debts. Dad strongly influenced us to put the money we were making back into the properties. We put on an extra couple of men and worked with them, mostly fencing or repairing fences, things that we had never been able to do before. We built sheds, and when tractors became available we put in big dams; we fenced them in, put up windmills and built troughs, and it increased the carrying capacity on a lot of our places by up to 30 per cent.

Of course, the shearers wanted to be in on this windfall as well. I agreed with them, because a lot of the cockies didn't know what to do with the money anyway—it virtually all went to the taxation department. The shearers quite rightly asked for a higher wage, and this was put forward by the Australian Workers Union (AWU). The arbitration court granted the shearers a 'wool value allowance' what became known as a 'prosperity loading', which was to be paid until such time as the wool prices went back down, and most of the graziers were quite happy to pay it. It wasn't a straight-out wage increase—it was a loading to be reviewed annually and which would be removed when wool prices dropped.

Wool prices, of course, did come down. By 1952 they had returned to half again of what had been received the previous year, and prices generally kept falling as the demands of the Americans waned. They fell again when the Korean War ended in 1953.

During the wool boom, we were organising sheds on the different places, paying off our debts and shearing our own sheep, and we would often get other local shearers to come out and give us a hand.

We used to get visits from the AWU organiser Peter McKitrick, who was based at Hughenden. When any shed was starting, the union blokes would come out, especially to the big sheds, and collect their dues. McKitrick would hear when we were shearing, and he'd come out to check that the shearers all had their union tickets. If shearers didn't have or wouldn't buy a union ticket, the boss or the organiser was supposed to sack him. Often, if the shearer didn't want to buy a ticket, the contractor or owner would buy him one, just so the shearer could be kept on and to keep the peace, and the shearer wouldn't know anything about it.

I got on with McKitrick. If I wasn't shearing on the team myself, I'd go in and shear a couple of sheep and let each of the shearers have a break, a chance to have a smoke. I'd have a yarn with them, and they saw me as a shearer, one of them, not just a cocky. McKitrick would go out and talk to them—usually at smoko, because then he'd get a feed as well.

The cook was paid by the owner or contractor. Usually the contractor would work out how much food they needed for ten to twenty men for two or more weeks, and the local storeowner would have it worked out per man per day and a big food order would arrive on the mail truck. Shearing was such a big business.

There were some bloomin' good shearers' cooks—they were tremendous. But the majority of them had a problem—most of them were alcoholics. I remember one bloke we hired. We knew he had a drinking problem, so we made sure there was no 'lemonade' (code for rum, as it used to be illegal to take alcohol to sheds) in the mess order. Somehow he still managed to get hold of some alcohol. We went through his swag and his quarters, but we couldn't find anything, and he was still getting drunk every day. We finally woke up to it—he was requesting a dozen bottles of essence of lemon in an order, when you'd probably only normally order one. He was drinking essence of lemon (which had an alcohol base) and was getting the DTs from it. Imagine drinking that. We had a lot of bindi-eyes that year around the quarters, and he'd get up in the morning and walk through them barefoot and not even notice.

We used essence of lemon for toothache as well, or oil of cloves. I've seen people use battery acid if the tooth had had it and they couldn't get to town—they'd place drops of the acid on the infected tooth to kill it.

Sometimes, if there wasn't a designated cook, one would be chosen by a vote from among the shearers and shed staff.

Keeping lots of good food up to hard-working men was an important job. If they didn't like the meals, it was common to hear someone yell out, 'Who called the cook a bastard?' with someone else replying, 'Who called the bastard a cook?'

In July, when shearing was in full swing, there were on average twenty-two teams in the Hughenden district, there were that many sheep to be shorn. Shearers relied on the graziers for work and the graziers relied on the shearers to get the wool off their sheep.

Chapter 22

Aeroplanes and eaglehawks

DAD WAS ONE of the real old bush horse people. He didn't like progress; he didn't even like us having jeeps or a truck— he reckoned we should have still been using our wagonettes and drays. So we could never understand it when he went and bought a plane in 1952. It was one of the few occasions when he really let his head go.

I think Somerset Airways had just started off in Muttaburra, about 75 mile north of Longreach. One time Dad got caught and he really wanted to go somewhere, so he rang them up. They came and landed right at MacFarlane, picked him up and took him where he wanted to go. In just a couple of hours he ended up somewhere that normally would have taken him a couple of days to get to.

Well, he could never stop talking about it. And he went straight out and ordered a plane. He was starting to get a few pound together after the wool boom and he had the money. But it was something that was so strange for him to do, to get this plane. As far as I know, he was the first grazier in the Longreach area to have one. Mind you, we didn't get around much in those times—we were too busy working at home—so there could have been others around that I didn't know about.

First he bought a Sky Jeep from England, sight unseen. It came from England in crates and was put together by mechanics in Brisbane, but they told us it wasn't suitable to fly in Australia, and especially where we would be flying. In real hot areas you want curved wings, to give the plane lift as the air passes over it, but the Sky Jeep had a real flat wing, which didn't give enough lift in hot weather. The flat wing made the plane fast when it was in the air, but getting it up there was the problem.

So the Sky Jeep was sold to someone in New Zealand; it worked there, because it wasn't as hot as western Queensland. Then Dad bought this single-wing Auster Super Autocar instead. It was all canvas covered—it looked a bit like a single-wing Tiger Moth, I suppose. It was noisy, slow and bumpy in rough weather. The thermals in our area could go up 300 to 400 foot in the air and then come crashing down taking the plane with it, and the Auster felt every shift, big and small.

Dad told me to go down to Sydney and get a pilot's licence. As soon as I got there I went to the doctor, but he wouldn't give me a medical to fly, because I'm colour blind. That was something I hadn't known until then, but for some time I'd known something wasn't quite right. When we'd be out shooting in really thick gidgee and brigalow scrub with a lot of grey kangaroos about, I'd often spot one and tell the others, and the boys would go, 'Where?' 'There!' I'd tell them. 'Can't you see?', but they couldn't see them. During the war they were apparently after blokes like me because camouflaging doesn't work when you're colour blind. The army was getting colour-blind people to spot out of planes any equipment hidden under camouflage netting, because they could see things better than cameras. You can camouflage what you like, it makes no difference to me—it's all just shades of grey. When I'm driving, I can only tell which traffic light is showing from its position, not from its colour. I won't drive in cities I don't know—there are lights everywhere and I don't know what they're for. I can usually see yellow, but everything else is just different shades of grey.

You couldn't get a pilot's licence if you were colour blind because all of the landing signals and so forth at controlled 'dromes were done with lights—red, yellow or green—and I couldn't tell the red and green apart. I had a few lessons, but I never actually got my licence which was a bit disappointing. Lach then went down to Sydney and got a licence instead. Pretty easy to get your plane licence then, unless you were colour blind.

At that time there were no radios in small planes; it was only later that UHF radios became commonplace in smaller planes. When you took off anywhere, even from your own place, you were supposed to phone the Department of Civil Aviation and tell them your destination, your departure time and how long you expected your flight to take, and give them a SARTIME (Search and Rescue Time), which was usually half an hour longer than your planned flight. SARTIME is still a requirement today. If you hadn't reported in by the scheduled time, they would be onto search and rescue very quickly. You were supposed to do this for all flights, but we didn't always. We couldn't very well ring in and say, 'Look, we're going shooting eaglehawks.'

On two occasions in my life I have seen eaglehawks getting joeys dropped out of a roo's pouch. On both occasions a mob of roos were heading across open downs with the heavy-laden does bringing up the rear. An eagle would fly along close beside the doe, almost touching her with its wing; then she would panic and ditch the joey, and the eaglehawk would have the joey as it hit the ground.

I have seen eaglehawks take bush turkeys twice. Eagle-hawk claws have three large toes in front and one very large toe behind. They would work in pairs, with the first eagle diving down from approximately 200 feet and ripping the hind toe of one of its claws along the turkey's back. Feathers would fly everywhere. Then the other eagle would do the same until the turkey fell down. The eagles then landed on the turkey. I saw this in the same area two years running, so it may have been a practice of those two eagles only.

At one stage we were having a lot of trouble with eagle-hawks taking lambs. When the ewes started lambing, the eaglehawks would just appear from nowhere. On the first day of lambing, we were bringing in about four thousand ewes and it rained, and we couldn't bring them all across the creek. So we had to leave about twelve newborn lambs with their mothers while we got the rest of the ewes across. When we came back, there were about twenty eaglehawks, some very distraught ewes, and every single lamb was dead. So they were a real pest.

Hugh in an eaglehawk nest with a young bird.

Lach and I were taking off one day on the strip at MacFarlane in the Auster and I said to him, 'You know, if I sat in the back seat and took that door off, I could shoot all those hawks with a shotgun.' It was no good shooting in the middle of the day, because the thermals that built up during the day with the heat would beat you and spoil your shot, so morning was best. We took the door off and gave it a try. We went up and shot about a dozen that day.

When the ewes next started lambing we got in the plane and shot about twenty eaglehawks in half an hour. They weren't protected then, but they are now of course.

On one trip we tipped the wing off an eaglehawk, took out the feathers at the end of the wing so he couldn't fly, and Lach went back and got it. He ended up being Lach's pet. Lach had him for years, and he was enormous—his wingspan would have been over six foot. He became real quiet and, as a joke, Lach even took him to the local show and entered him in the budgerigar competition as a Giant Western Budgie. Don't think he won.

We'd also get a dead sheep or rooster—anything at all to attract eaglehawks—and set up traps around the dead animal. We even used Lach's eaglehawk as a decoy a few times. We attached a chain to his leg and pegged him down with traps all around; the others would see him, come down to investigate and get caught in the traps.

Then we thought we'd try using the plane for shooting dingoes at Beatrice Downs. There were some hills a few miles off with a lot of stunted gidgee. We used to fly up and down this gidgee country and these dingoes would duck out of the scrub and I'd see them heading for the more heavily timbered hills; then we'd throttle down and come in low, and bang! We were only shooting from about 50 feet away and we never missed. We used an Icil Special SS, which has a real high-powered cartridge and it used to belt hell out of you with its recoil if you didn't know what you were doing. It was so deadly it just used to disintegrate everything.

One bloke heard through the local grapevine what we were doing, rang and told us, 'We're having trouble with a couple of dingoes and we can't get them,' so we flew down the 100 mile to his place. We were there ten minutes and got the dingoes that were eating his lambs. We'd go into the timber country and the dingoes would be trying to get back to the hilly country, and I'd tell Lach when I saw one, so we'd come in with plenty of flap on and at low speed, and bang! Then we got a bit of a reputation—'Get the Tindall boys, they'll get them for you.' If they could tell us roughly where a dingo was, we could usually find him. There was no heavy timber, it was all gidgee scrub; I could spot them easy enough, and being above them helped to see them better as well.

With the plane we could transfer men and materials from one place to another in just a matter of hours. It was great. It wasn't expensive—as long as the planes were used properly, they paid for themselves, especially in the wet.

Chapter 23

Aerial adventures

BY 1954, LACH and I had shifted onto the wether country near Hughenden. Together, us four boys had bought another block, Antrim, 48,000 acres, 60 mile south of the town. Because we were such a big family and had a track record of putting any money we earned back into the places and paying off our debt, it was quite easy going to a bank or an agent. We had a reasonably good name in that way, because we used to work hard and do our own work. Very little money changed hands—we would just mortgage one property against the other. The banks probably thought that if we went broke, everyone else in the district would have been broke too.

We now had five places—Red Knob, Beatrice, Thurles, MacFarlane and Antrim. Dad was still living at MacFarlane. One of our other brothers would be 100 mile away on one of the properties and would ring and want some sheep shorn, or lambs marked, and they'd want a couple of men. So Lach and I would get up before daylight, be down there in an hour or so, and then fly back at night. We used the Auster quite a bit. When Brian got his licence after he left school, Dad bought a Cessna—a Cessna 182, and that was really something.

Lach had a plane accident not long after he married Margaret in 1953, and she was in the plane with him when it happened. It was only a minor one, similar to a lot of the accidents that happened out there at the time. He went to land on an airstrip that was too short; he put the brakes on hard at the end of the strip and the plane went up on its nose. When the plane stopped, Margaret was upside down; she undid the seatbelt and fell down on her head, but she was alright.

There were quite a few minor plane accidents with people we knew; often it was just that they ran out of strip. People were starting to put strips on their places, but some were a bit rough. You should run a car up and down a strip before it's used, just to check it. If you could drive a car along it at 30 mile an hour, then you could land there, and it had to be a minimum of 200 yards long and about twenty foot wide, so you didn't have much margin for error. You can have a nice clean strip, but if it had a little bit of gravel on it and there was some light rain, it would act just like it was a wet road and the plane could skid.

We didn't use the plane to muster like some people did. A couple of times Lach would fly around to the back of the place and do a circle and the sheep would start running in, but that was about it. On some of the bigger places, they used to fly around mobs and then follow them, going backwards and forwards at the tail like you would on a horse, making sure none dropped off. One young bloke we knew got killed mustering in his plane.

Another young bloke we knew had his commercial licence and used to fly for a private company in Townsville. He'd taken these people who worked for the electricity company out when they were building the big power lines out of Townsville, and they wanted to get back to town and it was very stormy. He apparently didn't initially want to go, but they insisted, so they flew off, and didn't make it.

In the early 1950s, in what some people called the Golden Years of Wool, Wally and June Schultz owned Ventcher, a sheep property 40 miles south-east of Hughenden as the plane flies. It had probably the best and longest airstrip in the west. They owned a Leopard Moth plane, and every so often they would put on an open-day fly-in. There would be so many planes coming in to land, it was like moths coming to the light; there should have been a control tower there. On the open day they ran all sorts of competitions—landing on a marked spot and flour-bomb dropping. In another one the pilot would drop a toilet roll out of the plane, then put the plane into a roll to do a 180-degree turn, and finally cut the falling line of paper with the plane's propeller.

There were four people with planes within a 150-mile radius of us, and we could all be called upon in emergencies. Some of the strips weren't good enough or long enough for the bigger Royal Flying Doctor Service planes to land on. As long as you could land there, you'd go and help. It might be helping to get people to doctor appointments, or taking them into Hughenden or Longreach, where there was a doctor or necessary medical care. Lach would sometimes be called on at a moment's notice; a doctor would call and ask if we could get somewhere.

One time the doctor was with a woman who was having twins. He examined her and said she had to go to town now, and she wouldn't make it by car, so Lach was called out. He flew over to the property and landed; they put her in the back of the plane with the doctor in the front. According to Lach, the doctor was giving her instructions all the time. They had been in the air for only ten minutes when she said, 'I think it's too late.' She felt the babies were coming then and there. Lach sat there for a bit flying along and then leant back towards this woman and said, 'You can have one, but you're not allowed to have two.' The doctor looked at him, like 'What the hell are you talking about?' Lach looked at their two dumbfounded faces and explained with a smile, 'Well, this is only a four-seater plane—one baby will make four, another baby we'll be overloaded.' They had to laugh, but anyway, they made it to the hospital in time.

The planes were very useful. In a flood you'd ring around and say you were going to town in the plane, and did anyone want anything. Sometimes you'd be asked to get a bottle of 'lemonade' (you'd never say 'bottle of rum' on the party line). One bloke I knew would deliver the bottle straight out of his plane in the air. He'd get a big high-top loaf of bread, scoop the middle out of it and put the bottle in there; as he was flying low over the homestead isolated by floodwater, he'd throw it out. Rarely did the bottle get broken.

Ceb Barnes was a member of parliament who lived at Warwick in the Southern Downs area to the east, and one of his relations used to fly over us every now and again in a Tiger Moth. We were on the direct flight path between Winton and Hughenden. A couple of times Barnes' relative would be flying at about 1000 feet and he'd see us below, cut the motor and dive down on top of us and just open the throttle as he went overhead. The roar of this big engine would give us a scare. Once we had some visitors at Tambo and one of the women was having a shower out in the back shower block; when she heard that noise she thought the whole house was falling down, so she shot outside in the nude. She very quickly realised what had happened and went back in for a towel.

Another time, quite a few years later, a bloke I know was working at enlarging and smoothing an airstrip 90 mile north of Hughenden for the Flying Doctor to land on. He was using a big council dozer to improve it, but it was still pretty rough when this fellow Barnes landed his Tiger Moth on it. After a very rough landing coming in, Barnes knew he'd never get up the speed to take off again with the surface the way it was. So what he did was he got downwind with the wind behind him. The Tiger Moth doesn't have a tail wheel, it just has a skid, so he tied a rope onto the skid and tied the other end of the rope onto a log lying at the end of the runway. Then he told the dozer driver, 'I'll get in and have the engine flat out, and when I wave my hand you cut the rope.' And that's exactly what happened. This dozer driver said it was jumping up and down at full throttle, like a dog on a chain, and when the rope was cut it went straight up into the air and never turned a wheel.

I heard that when Barnes arrived back at the Hughenden airstrip later that day a pilot from a Fokker that had just landed was watching him coming in. He went over and asked Barnes, 'What the hell is that rope on there for?' There was still fifteen foot of cotton rope hanging off the skid at the end of the plane. Barnes apparently told the other pilot, 'Aw, you always tie tigers up by their tail, don't ya?'

Chapter 24

Splitting up and coming together

TINDALL AND SONS was starting to become a bit of a book-keeper's nightmare. How the accountant ever worked it out I'll never know. It had worked pretty well early on, but in 1955 we went our separate ways: Godfrey to Beatrice Downs; Arthur and his wife, Eva, to Thurles; and Lach, Margaret and I went out together and took over Antrim and started another partnership Tindall Brothers. Antrim could carry more stock than the other blocks and had good reliable water; it was worth more than each of the other blocks, so it was equitable that two brothers took it on. Dad still owned MacFarlane, and he sold Red Knob.

Antrim had channels running through it, a couple of mile each, following the direction the floodwaters ran. In a flood the water could come down fast from some low-lying hills nearby. The channels were dry most of the time, with coolabah trees along the banks. There were no permanent waterholes, but the channels could be ten foot at their deepest. The soil of the channels was erodible especially after a dry time, when the soil is so loose it will wash away if you get a lot of rain.

When it rains the soil consolidates and all the cracks close up and you get bogged when you drive around on it very easily. The worst bogging occurred when you got two inches of rain after drought. The rain just goes straight down into the crack, carrying the loose soil, and it gets real sloppy. At the end of the wet season it's usually easier to get around than at the beginning.

That country, where it opens up and then closes again, will actually lift the soil, so things like fence posts can be gradually lifted out of the ground a bit each year, half an inch at a time, until they all fall out. We would try to get out to the fences after a heavy storm and stand on the bottom wire either side of the post to push it back into the ground. Lach and I would do about three mile a day—pushing and wobbling on the bottom wire. But if you left it till the end of the wet season you couldn't do it as the ground would be firmer.

Mum and Dad stayed at MacFarlane and helped Brian buy a block, Gaza, at Isisford, south of Longreach. My sister Ethel became engaged to David Hardy and they wanted a place of their own, so they bought Verastone in the Muttaburra area, about 24,000 acres, and added onto it in later years. It was a very good property on high country with a good bore right at the house. We all still worked together and helped each other out at busy times, but ran our own places separately.

At this stage Brian and I were the only ones not married or engaged. Prior to splitting the partnership up, I had started to jokingly wonder if Dad was purposely sending me out to Beatrice every time I started liking or seeing a girl!

When I was about twenty-four, I used to go and see this girl who lived across the Vergemont Creek, Carmel Ballard. We eventually got engaged and I would ride over to see her and her parents; her father, Tom, was a drover of many years. Carmel's grandfather Alf had helped Dad with droving at Red Knob back in the 1938 drought.

Carmel was a marvel on the piano; she had a real musical gift. We'd hear these hit tunes once a week on the wireless, between six and seven at night, and she'd take down the music in her own style of shorthand. She'd type it up on the typewriter and then go and play it on the piano, and you'd think she'd been playing that song all her life.

When we became engaged, the Catholic priest at Longreach wanted to see me, and at Carmel's insistence I went. He started telling me what to do in the bedroom—I know what I told him to do and where to go. That put my new fiancée out and our relationship drifted a bit. We set a date for the wedding—not officially, just between ourselves and our families—but then put it off. We set another date and put it off again.

One time I rode over to visit Carmel and swam my mare across the river, swimming alongside holding on to the saddle, and didn't Tom go crook. He said, 'Never swim a mare.' I said, 'Look, we've swum them for years, no problem.' 'Don't matter,' he told me. 'Don't ever swim a mare—one day she won't swim.' As I've mentioned, a lot of the old drovers had come down the Georgina and Diamantina in the past and had told me and my brothers to never, ever, swim across with a mare, but we'd never listened to them. Now Tom Ballard, my father-in-law-to-be, was telling me the same thing, and I still didn't believe him.

But that day, when it was time to go, I rode the mare back to the place where we normally swam across; and when I slipped out of the saddle to swim alongside her, she just stopped swimming and started pawing at the water and tried to get on my back. As soon as you take horses into the water, you know whether they will swim or not: if they start grunting, almost a short groan, as soon as the water goes up over their girth, then you know they'll swim. So you just slip off them, still holding the reins; if you have a saddle on them, you take hold of the front of the saddle, and you just get pulled along with them. But this mare tried to turn around and she was striking out at me with her front feet. She managed to get her back feet on the ground, so she was sort of jumping in the air and trying to get on top of me. I abandoned her and swam off underwater so she couldn't see me. Then she got out of the water and went and lay on the bank.

I don't know what happened; maybe she sucked up some water. But she was right for me to get back on, so we went back to the Ballards' and didn't Tom give me plenty about it! I finally learnt: you swim a gelding, and lead a mare.

Chapter 25

Seeing the world

IN 1954 I saw an ad in the paper for a world trip. I thought, 'Why not?' I had all this money saved up from shearing over the years and was due a holiday. Brian came too. He was about twenty-two at the time and Dad and Mum paid for him, but I paid my own way.

When we were growing up, we always earned our own pocket money from shooting roos and dingoes and collecting dead wool. Dad had always been tight with money, because he knew what it was like to have none. When we went into a café, he would pay for his drink and we'd have to pay for our own—even Mum would have to pay for herself. If he owed you a penny, you didn't need to worry, you'd get it; and if you owed him one, he wanted it back. Dad never gave me one thing in his life other than advice; he guaranteed our money at the bank when we purchased property, but that was about all. He didn't have anything when we older boys were young, but he did when Ethel and Brian were growing up. They can't give you anything if they haven't got it.

In Sydney, Brian and I got on a boat, the *Fairsea*, and set off on this world trip. We called into Melbourne, Perth, Colombo in Ceylon (now Sri Lanka), and Madras (now Chennai) in India; but we had to get off for a day at Aden in Yemen because there was unrest between the English and the Egyptians over the Suez Canal. It had been suggested to us that the trip through the Canal in the summer heat was slow and hot, so Brian and I and a few other passengers decided to go on a driving tour to Cairo and meet up with the boat again at Port Said, at the end of the Canal. When we disembarked at the start of the Suez, there were soldiers everywhere with tanks and guns aimed at us. I went up to one of the soldiers and suggested he take his finger off the trigger because we weren't a threat; I was ignored, and it was very tense.

We hopped on a waiting bus and drove to Cairo. You know the backside of a cow? Well, that sums up Cairo. Parts of it were very rundown; the mudbrick and pisé huts lining the road were falling down, and people sat outside them with running open sores. I don't know if it was leprosy or what—could have been, I suppose. It was all pretty depressing. We saw the pyramids sitting on a sand hill and then headed to Port Said.

We caught the boat to southern Italy, took a train through Italy and France, then a ferry and train to London.

It was all a bit of a blur, but we had been held up a day before being allowed into the Suez Canal and had to meet up with the tour group, so we didn't stop anywhere on the way to London.

As soon as we made it to London, we headed back to the continent. We visited Amsterdam, Germany, Switzerland and Italy, then went back to France, Belgium and back again to London. I bought a Rolex watch in Lucerne, Switzerland. It had a blue enamel face, and I saw it in a display case and asked about it; the shop owner said it had been especially made for an American who hadn't come back to pick it up. I asked how long ago and they told me twelve months. I thought about it awhile, then went back and told them he wasn't coming back. It was a lot of money, but I never really bought anything like it before for myself, I had my shearing money and really wanted it; so I bought it. It is still going, but there is a tiny little chip on the face.

Back in London we went and watched cricket at Lords and tennis at Wimbledon. The day we saw the cricket it was bitterly cold and I had to buy a newspaper and put it down my shirt to keep warm. It was only a couple of days later when we went to Wimbledon and it was a beautiful warm day.

We then got on a boat from Southampton and crossed the Atlantic to New York. We saw the Statue of Liberty as we came into the harbour, and mobs of skyscrapers, including the Empire State Building. We went up to the top of the Empire State Building; it cost us a dollar, and you had to go up about three different lifts to get there, but it was worth it, looking down on this sea of buildings.

Then we got on a coach with about thirty other Australians and went to Washington. I think the road from New York to Washington was three lanes either side, six lanes altogether. I just couldn't believe it—there was that much traffic that they needed that many lanes. It was one of the most congested roads in America.

The bus drove us across to the west coast; we went through Chicago and Denver, and saw the Grand Canyon and Las Vegas casinos. That was something we'd never seen before. Brian and I went to a show in Vegas, and it was all boobs, bums and feathers. We went into a few of the big casinos. As I was walking up the steps of one, I saw a half dollar and picked it up; I went in and put it in the first slot machine I saw, pulled the handle and all this money came out. It was only about twenty dollars or something and the casino got it all back in about ten minutes, plus the half dollar I'd found. Other than sheep farming, that's about the extent of my gambling.

When we got to the west coast we got on another ship, the *Orantes*, at San Francisco and went to Honolulu and had four days there; we then went to Fiji and to Auckland and had a day there to look around, before making our way back to Sydney. I was a young fellow out seeing things I'd never seen before; it was quite an experience for a young bushy from outback Queensland.

When we arrived back in Sydney I saw the manager of Winchcombe Carsons, the agents who sold our wool, Mr Mountain—he was a big man too. He was just about to retire and he asked me what I was going to put my money into after seeing some of the world. I said it would still be sheep for me, but I told him to get into TVs and motels.

Australia didn't have any motels then; the first one that I knew of was in Townsville in 1955. Before that people stayed in pubs, and their cars had to be parked out on the street. There were no private facilities in pub accommodation, just a shared bathroom; in some of those big old pubs it could be 50 yards from your room to the toilet and the showers. I had seen how motels were working over there in America. There would be about thirty to forty of us, we'd pull up in our coach at a motel, all pile out, and go to our designated motel room.

Television was just coming in to Australia, getting ready for the Melbourne Olympics. Some of our motel rooms in the United States had TVs, and we'd always switch it on; you didn't have to head out at night to see the pictures, because they were there in your room. A couple of the Australians on the tour started to complain when there wasn't a TV in the motel rooms, they were getting so used to them. I could just see the possibilities that were there. I said to Mr Mountain, 'It's got to be motels, and television.' I told him to get into it now, and he'd make a fortune.

We were gone three months all up. It was quite an adventure for two brothers from Western Queensland in the 1950s. It was worth it—it was only shearing money anyway. I loved the whole trip; but I knew, when I returned, that I wouldn't want to live anywhere else in the world than Queensland.

Chapter 26

A broken strap

WE ARRIVED BACK in 1954, just before Ethel married David Hardy. One of Ethel's bridesmaids was Barbara Skelton. We were both in the bridal party but had different partners, because Barb was chief bridesmaid and the best man was a good mate of David's. My fiancé Carmel came along as a family guest.

I had first met Barb six or seven years before, when she'd come out to MacFarlane Downs with Ethel. They were at school together at The Glennie School in Toowoomba, and Ethel told her and some other friends to come home with her and meet her brothers, telling Barb, 'I've got a mob of them.' Poor Mum was at her wit's end—she still had four boys at home and now a whole lot of girls were visiting. She needn't have worried—nothing ever happened, never did in those times. I was born a generation or two too early, and what I wanted to do and what I was allowed to do were two

171

very different things; back then all you did was shake hands at the gate after you'd seen a movie or gone to a ball.

Ethel, Carmel, Ethel's friend Fay and Barb at MacFarlane Downs.

The first time Barb and I met was actually at about one in the morning. She'd come out from school with Ethel on the train; Mum had picked them up from Blackall, then they'd all gone to the movies. By the time they returned to MacFarlane Downs it was well after midnight.

I'd been down to Brisbane with a mob of sheep on the train. Back then, when you took a trainload of sheep or cattle to market, the railway would give you a return ticket free of charge so you could accompany and keep an eye on the stock. I'd left the Harley Davidson in Charleville; after I caught the train back, I had to ride the 150 mile or so back to MacFarlane that afternoon. I was pretty tired, because I hadn't had much sleep for a few nights, and I had gone straight to bed.

When they drove into the garage, Ethel saw my bike, knew I was back and decided she wanted to wake me up and show me something. The light went on; as I slowly woke up, I saw Ethel and this petite dark-haired girl standing in my room. Ethel introduced us; I was pretty tired but I still remember thinking Ethel's friend was a bit of alright.

Barb had three weeks there with us, and there were balls and races and all sorts of things going on, but we were all in a group, we didn't go out as couples. I was about twenty-three and Barb was only seventeen, and at that time I was seeing a nurse in Blackall.

Two years later, when Barb came back out for May week and the Longreach show, I realised how much she had grown up. There was an attraction, we both felt it, but she went home to Emerald, over 400 mile away from MacFarlane Downs, and I didn't have time to go all the way over there to go courting—there were mobs of animals to look after, and Dad kept sending me out to Beatrice.

After Ethel's wedding, we all went to a ball together, including Carmel. My relationship with Carmel was still pretty rocky, because I was anti-religious (still am). At this ball everyone danced with everyone else. The strap on Barb's dance sandal broke and it wouldn't stay on her foot so she couldn't dance anymore. She wanted to go back to the house and get another pair of shoes, and I offered to drive her. Well, the sparks flew. We only talked, but there was a definite connection and I wanted to get to know her better.

I'm a lot of things, but I don't two-time girls, so I officially broke it off with Carmel after that and we went our separate ways. After we broke up, Carmel married the manager of Dad's place, MacFarlane Downs. His name was Malcolm Barnfield and it was a bit awkward at first, but it was fine in the end. Malcolm and Carmel had four or five daughters, and the girls grew up and were really musical, and the family formed a band and they used to travel around playing music everywhere. Dad was a bit crook about it because they used to travel a lot, leaving early Saturday morning. But they were always back by Monday morning, and Malcolm always used to do his work.

In the early part of our romance, Barb was still living near Emerald with her parents and I was at Beatrice Downs, 310 miles away, which was not very satisfactory. I was too busy chasing dingoes, so I didn't have the time to go courting. Godfrey and his wife, Kath, were on Beatrice too, and someone had the idea that Barb should join us there for a couple of weeks so we could get to know each other better.

The next week she arrived and piled straight into the old Willys Jeep with me. The Jeep had no hood and it was loaded up with a water bag, a cut lunch, two dogs, a .303

rifle, ten dingo traps and a bottle of strychnine. We headed into the hills on Thurles Park. It was a very successful and romantic trip. I got the dingoes and Barb learnt to drive a jeep in the hills.

One afternoon at Beatrice, Barb and I went to tie up the dogs and collect the hen eggs for Kath. I had two big handfuls of eggs and I accidentally dropped one down the cleavage of Barb's dress while having a bit of a cuddle. I was so embarrassed and, in my hurry to retrieve it, I clumsily broke it. Egg yolk looks disgusting dribbling down someone's leg.

On that trip Barb told me she'd liked me from afar for a long while and she had even told her mother that she wouldn't marry anyone else until Hugh Tindall was married. I don't know if I ever did formally propose to her; we just took it for granted we were getting married. One of us suggested we should set the date, and less than a year later we were married. Barb still reckons she plucked me off the shelf.

Barb's people had a 24,000-acre cattle property right on the Nogoa River, twenty mile down from Emerald. I went over for the Christmas and we told her parents we were getting married. I hadn't met Barb's parents, but they knew all about me. We set a wedding date and Barb wore the engagement ring for the first time at the Church of England Easter Ball in Emerald. We were married on 24 September 1955—we both thought we'd waited long enough.

Engagement 1955

Lach and Margaret were already living at Antrim when Barb and I married. Luckily we all got on well, because for the first few years of our marriage we shared the same house. Built in about 1910, it was a huge old place with a kitchen block separate from the house, joined to it by a short walkway. Barb and I did up the kitchen block and lived in it and Lach and Margaret lived in the main house until they built their own place four years later, and then we had the whole place to ourselves.

Our telephone exchange was at Tangorin, out to the west, and it officially worked from nine in the morning to five in the afternoon, when the family who ran it manned the exchange. They were very good people. The exchange was in their house; if they were there, they would answer. If you just kept ringing they'd know it was an emergency and pick up, but you tried not to ring after hours if you could. However, at night was when most bushmen had time to make their phone calls, and at night you're supposed to pay extra.

Ten mile to the east of us was a party line to Hughenden which had six people on it. To save any problems in an emergency, we built a private telephone line the ten mile to our nearest neighbours, the Wearings at Elabe, who then had two phones sitting side by side. In an emergency we could ring the Wearings and they could pass on messages for us on their party line.

One day, Lach, Barb and I had gone somewhere in the Land Rover. Margaret was at home, and the jackaroo we had helping us out at the time, Vic Ward, raced over to the house in a bit of a flap. He had been in the long-drop toilet and he told Marg that a redback spider had bitten him. Marg asked him where. The bloke ummed and ahhed and Marg figured it must have been somewhere rather sensitive. So she rang Violet Wearing, who rang the local doctor on the party line, and he asked where Vic was bitten. Violet came back to Margaret, asking where he'd been bitten. So Margaret asked Vic, but he still wouldn't reply. The doctor insisted that he had to know exactly where Vic was bitten. Vic finally said, 'I was bitten on the left one.' So that went back to Violet, who told the doctor that he had been bitten on the left one. I don't know if anybody else was listening in on the phone by then or not, but, knowing party-line telephone conversations, they could well have been.

Then Lach, Barb and I arrived back, and Margaret raced out to tell us, 'The jackaroo's been bitten by a redback spider.' So Barb piped up, offering great bush wisdom: 'You've got to treat it like a snake bite—you've got to cut it and suck it.' And of course Marg just disintegrated in laughter and told us where he had been bitten. Barb never quite lived that one down.

Chapter 27

The 1956 shearers' strike

I WAS LISTENING to ABC radio one day in 2006 when I heard this bloke talking about the 1956 shearers' strike. He was a retired AWU bloke, and he either didn't know what he was talking about or he was flat-out lying. He said that the strike was caused by hungry graziers trying to take the shearers wages. I couldn't believe it. It was the removal of the 'prosperity loading' by the Federal Industrial Court and the state Queensland Industrial Court that caused the strike. The secretary of the Queensland AWU in Queensland Joe Bukowski said 'If I were a shearer I would not shear at the new rates,' while Bill Gunn, president of the United Graziers Association (UGA) told graziers 'you are in for the fight of your lives'. As far as the graziers were concerned the AWU had agreed to the removal of the loading once wool prices fell, it was a way to share the profit of the wool boom, and the boom was over.

179

So I got onto the ABC and told them, 'You find out your facts.' I was thirty years old in 1956; there aren't many of us left who lived in the bush then and were really involved with the shearers' strike.

They sent me the tape; I got the facts and sent it down to them and had a quick interview over the phone, which was aired the following day on the ABC. That night our phone never stopped ringing with people from out west, and they all agreed with me.

In 1956 every large town had a branch of the UGA; it was based in Queensland and represented farmers, mostly sheep and cattle graziers. At the town branch meetings, local grievances and suggestions would be debated and forwarded on to the district branches; if they thought there was merit in any of the suggestions, they would go on to the state branch to be voted on. We had decided to join the UGA after the war. Our branch was Hughenden, our district was South Western Queensland, and Brisbane was the state office. Issues could be around water, feral pests, land management, anything that the government could be lobbied on.

By 1954, wool prices had dropped considerably. So the UGA went back to the arbitration court and asked for the prosperity loading for shearers to be abolished. The court granted the UGA their request and did away with it, mostly because the price of wool had come down and costs had risen so much with the higher wages. As of 1 January 1956, the loading was abolished.

The shearers weren't going to work for less, and the graziers no longer wanted to pay the old, higher rate. So it caused a very vicious strike between the graziers and the shearers: the 1956 shearers' strike.

Everyone wanted a part of the golden egg that was the wool boom, and then the egg broke.

Our family now had six properties altogether—Beatrice, MacFarlane, Thurles, Antrim, Verastone and Gaza—but we owned them, and ran them, separately. By then we were shearing about a hundred thousand sheep a year between us. Before the strike, I shore alongside my brothers and other shearers in teams on all the properties. I used to go from place to place shearing lambs, rams and stragglers and organising shearing teams.

You crutched at the beginning of the year, and usually by July travelling shearers would come north to work around Longreach and Hughenden and start shearing their way south, finishing in Victoria and then slipping across the Ditch to New Zealand. You also had the local shearers in the towns, who would shear around the district for about six months.

Most places started crutching by February, as it cooled down, mostly getting in the local shearers. But in 1956, with the shearers on strike and a warm damp season, sheep were being struck by fly and dying in their thousands. By March, sheep graziers were seriously worried. I was already a pretty good shearer before the strike started, but I was about to get a whole lot more practice.

Nineteen fifty-six had been another big flood year. Heavy rain fell in the wet season, causing flooding, but then it continued raining through to April—nuisance rain, with a cyclone on the coast. All the rivers stayed up. I had been crutching and shearing in our own sheds, because of the floods and the threat of fly strike in our sheep. My brothers and I then shore all our own sheep, and as the strike dragged on we started helping some neighbours out. At the beginning of April, you still couldn't get around the district much at all, except in four-wheel drives, because of the floodwaters; but there were a handful of planes around the district by then—if airstrips were out of the floodwater, the planes made it quick and easy to go between places.

Three UGA blokes—Bill Gunn, Peter Bell and Mick Leake, who was more or less our neighbour—came up to a meeting in Hughenden for anyone interested in what was going on and said, 'We gotta do something about this.' Bill Gunn was from Goondiwindi, down near the New South Wales border. I had known him through the UGA for ten years before the strike. He was a good organiser and a forceful speaker. He would travel out to UGA meetings all around the state, talking about what the UGA was up to. A big man in more than just size, he liked to get things done. He had flown some shearers over from New Zealand at the start of 1956, to get his own shearing done. The shearers didn't have as strong a union over there as in Australia, and they were happy to come over and work. The Kiwis were given a hard time by the Aussie shearers as they were considered 'scabs', but for us trying to get the wool off our sheep, they were saviours.

Bill, Mick and two others started organising shearing teams in Longreach, Blackall, Cunnamulla and Charleville. Western and Central Queensland had already been the site of vicious shearers' strikes in the past, and the feeling in the towns between shearers and graziers was pretty black at this stage. The teams they were organising had quite a few local sons of graziers, as well as cockies, jackaroos, station hands, and shearers from New Zealand. Unlike the Kiwis, the jackaroos didn't get into trouble with the striking shearers as they weren't officially shearers, they just worked on the properties.

I was asked by Bill Gunn to start organising sheds around Hughenden. I was already sort of half running these sheds anyway, to shear our own and neighbours' sheep, and they asked me if I could organise more teams and start the ball rolling. I organised one team and then another. I would be on the phone at night, ringing around different people, organising a team for the next day, up to the next week, at all the different places in the area. I used to try and keep a full board of shearers going all the time. You'd organise one bloke to go one day and another bloke to go the next, because none of them were full-time shearers and often they had other jobs on their own places that needed doing. They would ring me up and say, 'I can be there Monday

183

and Tuesday, but I can't be there Wednesday.' The roustabouts were fairly easy to get; I organised blokes to do that
who couldn't shear, or who were too old to shear.

With all the organising our phone bills cost a bit. If
you called after five in the afternoon you were supposed
to pay extra, but most workers you couldn't ring before
five. Mrs Buntine at the Stonehenge exchange was pretty
good—she'd often put your call through and go and have
a cuppa, and come back later and check if you were still
on the line.

I was organising people from all around the district to
go to different sheds. As long as we could land the plane, we
could transport the shearers around. I was mostly shearing
around Hughenden, but I went down to Tambo as well. We
were too busy with sheep in our area to really go anywhere
else. Lach and I started shearing full-time in other people's
sheds on the first Monday in April, and continued until the
strike broke in early October—we went away five days a
week, and would come home to our farm work and families
for the weekends.

Every week, sometimes two or three times a week, I'd
get a new learner that had to be taught to shear. Some of
the cockies and their sons could shear a little bit—enough
to tidy up or crutch a single sheep—but they couldn't really
shear sheep after sheep, day after day. So I'd get in the
middle of two learners, and I'd be shearing and teaching the
two learners at the same time. I'd show them how to start,
how to move their feet, how to get the comb right down on

the skin and keep it there, not to hang about in the wool. You want to hold the handpiece as light as you possibly can, because it'll follow the skin that way. If you can shear clean, usually you can shear fast, because you're right down on the skin and that is where the best cutting is. If you're too high in the wool, the machine heats up and becomes too hot to hold comfortably.

Up until April that year the sheep were very hard shearing—the wool had gone green with all of the moisture and it wouldn't comb. But after the rains stopped in May, the wool started to lift and we could get into the wool underneath. We were getting the green wool off the sheep, but if it was still damp, we had to put the fleeces out to dry. You can't press wet wool.

Not only was it hard to shear some of the sheep because they had green wool after too much rain, but some of them had fourteen to sixteen months' wool on them by the time we got to them. We thought we just wouldn't be able to keep up with all the work, but the new shearers got better as time went on. They became faster and we became better at organising the teams.

Bill Gunn would ring me at night and ask what was going on, how we were going. I became the organiser for the Hughenden region with the help of a bloke by the name of Percy Taft, who was the manager of Grazcos (the Graziers Co-operative Shearing Corporation) in Longreach at the time. I couldn't handle the organisation of the real big sheds, with twenty or more shearers. So Grazcos ran those sheds, or the owners just had to pay the higher rate to the union shearers to get their sheep shorn.

Originally an organisation of graziers, Grazcos became a giant shearing and wool company. It was well supported by wool producers over the years, as it also had a wool pooling turnout in Brisbane: if you had a lot of star lots or lines—small lots of wool—they'd sort it all down in Brisbane and class it into bigger lots, making it more attractive for buyers, and you'd get a better price that way, even with Grazcos doing the sorting. They'd get wool from us and some more from Joe Blow, and they'd make a three or more bale line of it and get a much better price.

Percy had helped Dad in 1952, when the AWU had taken him to the Industrial Court in Tambo over conditions. It had been a ridiculous business. The AWU bloke in Longreach was a real bastard. He had come to the house one day and wanted to see the shearers' wages book; when Mum showed it to him, he called her a liar, that it wasn't correct. Well, Dad hit the roof. He demanded the AWU bloke leave the house, and gave him a kick up the seat of his pants as he went through the door for good measure.

The AWU bloke wanted to take Dad to court for assault, but the union wouldn't go for an assault charge. Instead, they took Dad to court over a hole in the gauze of our meat house—not the shearers' meat house—where a bird or something must have flown into it. You don't leave holes in meat houses, it makes no sense with flies around, it makes it unsanitary and if we had seen it before the AWU bloke, it would have been fixed for sure. Dad was fined ten pounds. He didn't think much of the AWU after that.

Chapter 28

Ducks on the pond and handpieces

JUST AFTER THE strike started, Barb and I found out we
were expecting our first baby, and we were so happy. Even
though she was pregnant, Barb still came and helped out in
the sheds when we were short of workers, like a lot of the
women. They used to joke that she was the first pregnant
roustabout any of them had seen. As she got bigger with the
pregnancy she found she couldn't bend over to pick up the
fleece, so she just swept the board and kept it clear of wool
for the shearers.

It was a funny thing: up to 1956, women weren't even
allowed in the shearing shed in Australia. If a woman
came into a shed or was seen heading towards one,
whoever saw her would call out, 'Ducks on the pond,'
letting everyone know a woman was on the way and to
curb their language. Even though the woman might have
owned the place and owned the sheep, she more or less

had to ask the shearers if she could come down and have a look at the shearing.

I shore with a couple of women during the strike, a couple of Kiwi women at the end of 1956, and they were good shearers. A few of the Hughenden graziers' sons had gone over to New Zealand to find shearers, and probably a third of the teams over there were women. So they brought these girls back with the blokes to work in the sheds. Separate amenities for the women were a problem to start with, but we soon worked it out. There are plenty of female shearers in New Zealand, and now of course they're not that unusual out in the bush here either.

Up until 1956, the handpieces had always been supplied by the graziers, because otherwise the shearers would grumble about someone else having a better handpiece than they did. A better handpiece—one that went well all the time, running easily, clean and cool—might be worth two or three sheep per run. Because the shearers were paid per sheep, that could add up. So the shearers weren't allowed to carry their own handpieces; the grazier would have to supply them.

When the shearers went onto the board, at each stand there would be a handpiece, an oil pot filled with clipper oil, a brush and a short screwdriver used to change and tighten the combs and cutters. When handpieces were supplied in the bigger sheds, an 'expert' would be employed by the shed as well, at the cost to the owner. The expert used to grind the combs and cutters. If there were any problems with the overhead gear in a big shed, an expert used to step in and fix it, but now it's up to the organiser or owner.

The shearer had to buy their own combs and cutters, but they used to get an allowance as part of their wages—two shillings or so per hundred sheep shorn—for wear and tear on the combs and cutters. You had different combs for different shearing: if you were working on really free-cutting sheep, with soft clean wool that comes off easily, you kept your points pretty sharp, but if they were hard going and you were likely to pick up skin, you used worn-down combs with more rounded points. You used your really good combs first and wore them out a bit on really fast-cutting sheep; then you changed them and kept the worn-down combs for harder-cutting sheep so the chances of nicking the skin as you make your way through the matted wool is reduced. You probably had three different degrees of wearings on your combs and cutters—especially your combs, more so than your cutters. Nowadays the shearers grind their own combs and cutters themselves. In the past an expert was hired to look after the handpieces and grind the combs and cutters.

Clipper oil is a real fine oil. It's mainly used to lubricate the moving parts inside the handpiece. Shearers will put a little oil onto the combs and cutters to start with, but too much oil will combine with the wool grease so that wool builds up under them. If you held the handpiece out and left it running, your comb and cutters would burn and get buggered. But as long as you're cutting, the grease in the wool is enough to lubricate them.

If there was a dozen shearers, they'd have a dozen extra handpieces. Sometimes, shearers being what they are, there'd be a better shearer on the board and they'd think they could keep up with him. If they couldn't keep up with the gun shearer, they'd reckon there must be something wrong with the handpiece. So they'd call the expert and get another handpiece, and the expert would go and grind their combs and cutters again.

Shearers might go to one shed and have a really good handpiece there, supplied by the owner, and when they left, the handpiece would sometimes disappear with them. They were fairly expensive—they're about four hundred dollars or more to buy new now; in those times they were twenty or thirty pound each. That was another reason they wouldn't allow a shearer to carry his own handpiece—most likely it wasn't his anyway. You weren't allowed to carry your own handpiece for years until 1956. I had my own special hand-piece after that and I wouldn't lend it to anyone.

Chapter 29

Scabs

AFTER A FEW months, the case went back to the arbitration court. Because the strike was dragging on, the court went halfway and granted the shearers a new rate that was halfway between the higher old rate that had included the loading and the new rates.

Instead of improving the strike situation and the shearers going back to work, this created a lot of ill feeling. The shearers stayed out, wanting more money, and there was bad feeling between graziers because some of them had to pay the higher money to get their sheep shorn and they got snooty. The longer the strike went on, the harder it became for the shearers; some were getting strike relief from the AWU, but it wasn't much. A lot of them were out of work for six months, with families to feed and little or no money; there weren't many other jobs in those western towns, and they just had to go back to work. Some of them would go out into the teams organised by the graziers and Grazcos. They'd sneak out to the working shed at night so no one could see them; once shearing started, the graziers wouldn't allow anybody—no union organisers or anybody else unknown to them—onto their place. Gates were locked, shotguns at the ready.

It got a bit bad in town, but not as bad as it did during the shearers' strikes of the 1890s, when the troopers had to be called in. There were fights between the shearers—anyone found to be shearing in a non-union shed was openly called a scab and given a hard time; their family was picked on in the street, or anywhere they went. Their kids were even picked on at school.

The strike kept on. The AWU ignored the wages commission, even when on 30 June the award went up again to above the pre-strike rate, as a wage increase. The shearers kept striking, and the graziers who didn't want to pay yet another increase to shear their own sheep. Some sheds agreed to pay the higher rate, to get the shearers there, but not all.

By the middle of the year, the shearers who depended on the work and never went out of their own town or district to shear—the same blokes I'd been shearing with for the last ten years—approached me very quietly to ask about work in the non-union sheds. I told them of course they were welcome to come out with us, and we could guarantee there wouldn't be any talk about it. If they wanted to shear, I'd have a pen there for them. Of course, when they went back into town and if they were found out they were called scabs, and the fights that went down between them were pretty bad.

As well as paying tax, the shearers who were being paid the higher rate were having to pay into a strike fund to support the out-of-work shearers. They were unhappy because the scabs were paid cash in hand, so even though they were earning a lower rate per hundred sheep shorn they were taking home more than the union shearers. There was plenty of hard feelings; the police were called out a lot. There were big fights, a lot of skin knocked off. It was a very nasty turnout. Owners, station hands and managers weren't considered scabs, so if they went into town they weren't picked on in the same way that the Aussie shearers that were working in the non-union sheds or the New Zealand shearers were.

There were five pubs in Hughenden, and the shearers drank at one and the graziers at another. One pub was housing scab shearers and had black paint thrown along its walls—it was blackballed. I heard the term 'blackball' came about from the gentlemen's clubs in London—when they were voting in new members, you put a white ball in if you wanted them to join, a black ball if you didn't. The black paint was thrown to show the scabs they weren't wanted.

The police didn't do anything they didn't want to. I know of a fight between shearers in Tambo one time when someone rang the police and they didn't come for half an hour. Unless there was a knife or there was danger of someone being killed, they'd arrive later and ask, 'What's been going on here?' I think they thought: why should they have to join a scuffle between a couple of big burly shearers or graziers?

In the 1891 and especially the 1894 shearers' strikes, big shearing sheds had been burnt down—places like Nive Downs near Augathella, which was burnt down on April Fools' Day in 1891. Sheds, wool and even sheep in sheds were burnt. It had got so bad that on some of the bigger places in western and Central Queensland they had armed guards on places twenty-four hours a day. (More information about these strikes is included in Appendix 3.) But in 1956 it was mainly grass that was burnt—they 'let the red steer go', as the saying went. But there was also one pub burnt that I know of in Hughenden, which I think, funnily enough, was the shearers' pub.

I wasn't personally attacked; I had no problem at all. I knew all the local shearers and had worked with most of them, and before the strike they always liked coming to my place and being in the teams I organised. The AWU man, Peter McKitrick, was a decent enough bloke and he knew what I was doing, organising non-union sheds. He'd seen me go down the board before the strike and do a few sheep for each shearer, to give them a blow or a break, that sort of thing. I guess by helping out like that it changed my status from being 'one of them' to 'one of us'.

Chapter 30

Black wool

BARB WAS PREGNANT all through the shearers' strike. There was a bloke came round one day, when Barb was about six or seven months pregnant—I think he may have been a sales rep or a traveller; anyway, Lach and I were away shearing of course. He called in and asked Barb if I was home and she told him I was away. Marg was also home, and she too was pregnant. He went into town afterwards and called into the agents. He said he wanted to see one of the Tindall blokes and the manager said, 'You won't find them at home—they're away working in the sheds, shearing. They're away all the time.' And this other bloke apparently said, 'Well, there must have been someone around at some time, because there are two very pregnant ladies out there.'

Barb went and stayed in Emerald with her parents for the last part of August and most of September; I was shearing nearly all the time anyway. And then for the last couple of weeks of her pregnancy she went to Rockhampton to be closer to the hospital. I went over at the very end of September and stayed with her parents. Our first baby, Maree Anne, was born on 2 October 1956. It was a difficult labour for Barb, but our new little girl arrived safely into the world, our little shearers' strike baby.

The strike continued. Nearly seven months in, the unions declared all wool was 'black' if it hadn't been shorn at the higher rates. Everybody knew everyone else—shearers knew each other, how many kids they had, even the dog's name—so they knew which sheds were working and if they had union shearers or not.

When they declared the wool black, it couldn't be transported on the trains, as the railway workers went on strike and refused to load the wool. So instead it was put onto trucks and the graziers took their own wool down to Brisbane to the woolstores. The railway lost millions. Some trucks were ambushed and their loads thrown out onto the road and drivers attacked, but most made it through. But then the workers went on strike down at the woolstores and wouldn't load out the black wool, so trucks were left sitting at the stores.

The UGA knew I was with Barb and our new baby in Rockhampton and that I wasn't shearing, and they asked me to go to Brisbane to help unload the wool. There must have been about twenty-five of us that went down—blokes from Cunnamulla, Hughenden, Longreach, everywhere—but I only knew three of them at the start. There were blokes from New Zealand as well. The woolstore owners were paying for our accommodation at a nearby pub, and paid us wharfie wages while we were there.

The woolstores were over 300 by 300 feet or 100 metres square—you can still see them on the river, but some have been converted into big offices and luxury units. They had these big doors to drive trucks in, and it was all open, no fences; they could stack up thousands of bales of Australian wool. It was going all over the world—Japan, Italy, China, England and America.

We used to meet at Winchcombe Carsons or Dalgetys at seven in the morning. The first few times we went down they took us in a special bus, but from then on we made our own way down; we generally walked, as it was only about half a mile. The first time we walked down, Jack De Kloote from Marmboo in Longreach and I were in the front of the line, and in each hand we had a steel wool hook, which was used to move the heavy bales around. The police had to give us an escort because of the striking wharfies lined up outside the store. The police said to us, 'You'll have to walk through them all. Whatever you do, don't look at them. Don't say anything, just keep on walking. You'll be right.' Imagine someone trying to attack you when you've got two wool hooks! He wouldn't stand much chance—you could grab him with one hook and rip his guts out with the other. Not that you would, of course. We got yelled at and I held my hooks in front of my face, so they could see them as we walked through. Funnily enough, there were no takers.

Instead of taking two hours to unload the wool trucks like the wharfies used to do, we could do it in half an hour. Then we were just sitting around playing cards, playing table tennis, walking up and down on the wharves having a look around—there was nothing to do. Then they'd give us lunch money; the pie bloke would come along sometimes or we could walk over to a café for something to do. Talk about a bludging job. Sometimes another truck would come in at eight o'clock at night, and we'd get overtime to sit there and wait to do half an hour's work.

After a while the blokes who were working the dump press also went out on strike, so we took over that job as well. We just had to load the wool bales in the big dump press; you'd put one or two ordinary wool bales in and compress them into about a third of their size, so they'd take up less room on the boats. We used wool elevators to lift the compressed wool up onto the highest parts of the rows: 336 pound some of them weighed 400 pound for bellies, locks and pieces. It was the easiest work—there was nothing to do most of the time except talk and play cards.

The next thing, the wool loaders—the blokes who loaded the wool into the boats—went on strike, and we said, 'We've got nothing to do, we may as well load the boats as well.' So we were unloading trucks, compressing the wool *and* loading the boats, each of us doing the work of three men. This all happened in ten days.

Then, as soon as we started loading the wool, the seamen went on strike. They said, 'Even if you stick it on the boats, we're not going to shift the boats.' By this stage, the Labor premier of Queensland had had enough: the state was going broke, and he stepped in, telling them that the alternative was letting in international carriers. Well, letting international carriers come into Australian ports and cart the wool meant they'd bring their own labour, instead of using Australian labour. It'd go onto international boats and all the Australian sailors would be out of a job. The whole strike came to a very quick end then: they called it off in less than twenty-four hours.

After the shearers' strike in 1956, I had the most money I'd ever had in my life. We were paid cash, and I ended up with a bloomin' cupboardful of money and I didn't know what to do with it. When we were shearing out at someone's place, on the Friday of every week or when shearing was finished, the owners of the place would go into town and get a port, small suitcase full of money to pay us.

By September I had a sugar bag full of cash. In October, when I finished at the wharves and was back home, I bought a brand-new Holden car, a Holden Special. I'd never had a new car before in my life. I paid the money into the bank and went down to Brisbane and picked up the new car. With the strike, a new baby and a brand new car, 1956 was quite a year.

Chapter 31

Life in the sheds

IT HAD BEEN challenging work keeping the shearing teams going all the time during the strike, but I really enjoyed it. Even though the strike ended in October, it was hard work right up to a couple of days before Christmas with the backlog of sheep still needing to be shorn.

There was one shed at Barenya at Hughenden—I think they had eight stands there. They were an older lot of shearers and they couldn't see themselves finishing before Christmas, so they asked me to come back and shear. Because there weren't any free stands, I set up a little one-stand plant on a 44-gallon drum and I used to have to drag each sheep out of number one pen and up another ten to twelve feet to where I was set up, and then afterwards let them go out through the engine room.

There was a big Maori bloke there and he was a very good shearer. We just went sheep for sheep day after day with these big wethers; we were shearing forty-four to forty-five sheep each per run, but they were beautiful shearing. Great big wethers, fourteen months' wool and very fat, and their wool was clean—hadn't had a spot of rain on them since April. After ten days we finished up tallying exactly the same number of sheep. The last run on the last day we both shore forty-two sheep in one hour thirty-two minutes. Neither of us could have kept up that pace all day. By the end of 1956 I was able to shear two hundred sheep a day with a narrow comb (which was slower than the wider combs that came in later)—I was shearing fit.

In a shearing shed there is always a fair bit of story-telling and prank playing that goes on. You'd have a great mob of blokes sitting around, remembering and retelling stories. The thing with shearer tales was, when they were in the sheds the stories were about the women they'd had, and in town the stories were about how many sheep they'd shorn. Usually both stories had a fair bit of exaggeration attached to them.

At the Barenya shed that year we had a young bloke working with us and we told him not to wander off down the river, because there was a black camp down there and they'd get him. We told him the aboriginal women would cart him off. So of course he went down the river looking for them and couldn't find any camp. That night we were all sitting around playing cards and had a laugh or two at the young fella's expense.

*

Originally shearers weren't allowed to bring any grog out shearing; if they did they could be sacked immediately. I don't drink at all, never have. I tried, but I just didn't like it—it used to make me sick. I won't even drink Coke.

But the blokes I was working with in 1956, mostly graziers' sons and jackaroos, would knock off for the afternoon and they'd be into the rum bottle or grab a beer. We were all shearing a lot of sheep at the time. Some of the other graziers could shear a bit, but it was harder on them than it was for me because I was used to it. Then at night they'd sit up to ten or eleven o'clock with the whisky and rum, and in the morning half of them would still be blotto.

Just after the strike I brought up at a UGA meeting in Hughenden that I didn't think it was fair that shearers weren't allowed to bring grog onto a place. I suggested that refrigerators be allowed in shearers' quarters. Now why not? Shearers are men, just the same as anyone. Other men work on council or have an office job and when they knock off they can have a beer. I explained that I let them on my place. But didn't I get into trouble for bringing it up!

The classer and the expert usually had a little two-bedroom area known as 'the boss's quarters', and the shearers had the other quarters. I was the first person I had ever heard of to put a fridge in the boss's quarters; any shearer could put as much alcohol as he liked in there. Come six o'clock, they'd be all sitting around with their beer, and the boss, usually the classer, would keep an eye on things.

A few of the blokes at the UGA meeting objected to me allowing grog in sheds. I let them talk, and then I stood up and pointed at three different blokes and told the meeting how when I'd worked with them during the strike they were too drunk to shear the next morning. 'Why can't a shearer, who works just as hard as you, have a drink?' I asked. 'If he's close to town, he can hop in his car, drive to town and go to a pub—why shouldn't he be allowed to have a drink on your place? If he's drunk, you can sack him, and I could have sacked the three of you.' I reckoned the shearers deserved a drink when they knocked off; if the owner thought they'd had too much grog, they could just sack them without the slightest turnout. I really got into trouble over suggesting that, but it was put up at the Longreach meeting of the UGA and it was eventually carried.

It's frowned upon to bring grog onto a place, even today, but they do. Some of the shearers have a special fridge for their grog to have after work, and why shouldn't they? Anyway it's changed now, which is good.

By February 1957 we started crutching again and I also continued going to a few places to shear. Rockwood was a fairly big stud depot seventy miles south of Hughenden, and they used to bring a lot of rams up from New South with full wool so people could have a look at the wool; then Lach and I used to go over there and shear their special stud rams. We sheared at a couple of other places as well, but no really big sheds.

By July 1957, there were twenty-two shearing contractor teams back working out of Hughenden for the year's shearing. Each team had a minimum of four shearers, but usually six shearers, plus six other men. Some sheds were even bigger than that. Then you add the roustabouts, wool pressers, classers, experts and cooks, making about a hundred and thirty men who'd go out shearing in July.

That year, 1957, I suggested in a UGA meeting that we should put on a shearing competition at the local show. They thought that was a wonderful idea. As I'd organised so much the year before, they reckoned I could organise that too. Me and my great ideas!

I had never heard of such a competition before, let alone run one. To make a stage I asked one of the local truckies to put two semitrailers side by side and as close together as possible. We put sheep on one and two electric shearing stands on the other. A local shearing contractor was one judge, AWU rep Peter McKitrick was another, and I was the third.

The three of us then set up a scorecard. We set a fairly fast time to shear three sheep each, so the shearers had to work quickly and efficiently. If their time was over our set time, so many points were lost per second; there was no advantage for time under the set time unless it was a dead heat. Points were lost for skin cuts, wool left on, bad handling of sheep, torn fleeces, second cuts and bad cuts, and a bad belly button or pizzle cut on the wethers was a no score. They were allowed one sheep each as a warm-up. The whole thing was a bit bushie, but from then on there have been a lot of tremendous shearing competitions around the country. All good fun.

Chapter 32

Sheep killers

AFTER THE 1956 floods, there was an explosion in the fox population. We shot over one thousand foxes that year—I know 'cause we took them into town and were paid a bounty of five shillings per head. We'd be going out at night with a big spotlight and getting thirty to forty at a time.

We'd skin the pelts but there were some lousy and stinking ones, as foxes often are, so once we shot them we'd throw them in the back of the ute; when we came to a big log we'd take them out of the tray and chop their head off on the log, wrap wire around their muzzle and hang them out a couple of mile from the house along a fence line to dry out. Instead of having to scalp them, which took time and was a stinking business, you could do the whole lot in five minutes and leave them there for six months to dry out. We kept the better skins to sell, but didn't bother when they were stinky and mangy.

Once the heads were dried out we'd take them to a receiver, which was sometimes the police station, sometimes the council, and tip bagfuls of dried heads out for them to count. They still smelt, but not as badly as when they were first shot; the receiver would kick the heads over with his boot one at a time to count them, and then we'd get paid. Definitely worth the trip into town with the stinking lamb killers.

Drying fox pelts, 1957.

Lach and I were running the waters one day, checking the bores and troughs, and we came across a large pig eating a roo carcass that I had shot the week before. We used to get two shillings (or about twenty cents) from the council for feral pig snouts and tails, so I went to get my two shillings.

Just as I got to him, he jumped up and gored me in the leg with his tusk. It was a big gash so I went immediately in to the Hughenden hospital. I was told not to touch or unbandage it for a week.

About three nights later, Barb and I had to pull the blankets up tight under our chins to stop the smell. It had gone rotten. After that I would unbandage it and sit in the sun for an hour a day at lunch and it eventually dried out and healed, but I still have a scar to this day.

As happens so often in the bush, droughts follow floods. Nineteen fifty-nine was a bad drought year. We were getting short of feed and I took about eight thousand sheep up onto Dutton River outside of Richmond and onto part of the Flinders watershed, and I didn't realise there were so many dingoes out there. I should have known better, because the owner, who had quite a lot of sheep, used to keep them away from the river. That should have woke me up that something was wrong.

The river was at least 200 yards wide, surrounded by deep thick sand; I saw a couple of dingo tracks there, but the owner had said he didn't have trouble with dingoes. I used to go out and check the sheep regularly, usually once a week. I was out one day and I saw this dingo. I shot it and it had a great belly, and I thought, 'It's full of pups.' After I scalped it, I opened it up and pulled out nine pups. I had never heard of nine; I'd seen them getting around with four or five bigger pups, so whether they don't all survive or they eat them or what, I wouldn't know.

Still, the problem wasn't so much the dingoes as the speargrass. There was one single patch of black speargrass in the middle of this paddock, but I never thought the sheep would go into it with so much other grass around. I learnt the hard way.

The next visit out there, I saw a single sheep standing by itself and not shifting and I thought, 'What the hell's gone wrong here?' I looked further and there were more of them, all standing still by themselves. I soon worked out when I had a good look at them that they'd gone into the speargrass and had the barbs in their skin. The speargrass makes it's way slowly through the wool as the sheep moves around, and it can't come out as it has a barbed end; then it works its way through the skin over time and up to an inch into the muscle of the sheep. The poor things.

I had eight thousand mostly aged wethers, four thousand of our own and four thousand of our neighbours'. All I could do was get them in and shear them, even though they had only six months' wool on them; at least it got rid of the majority of the spears. After shearing them I had to get rid of the sheep with bad speargrass contamination; they were condemned to the meatworks, but because the speargrass formed abscesses in the meat, they went for dog food, not human consumption.

I have since heard that years ago, in the early 1870s, they had this black speargrass growing north of Charters

Towers. One early settler by the name of Hann took twenty-four thousand sheep up there, but between the Aborigines, the dingoes and the speargrass, they soon realised it wasn't sheep country. So they decided to take them south. You couldn't travel twenty-four thousand sheep in one mob, so they split them into four. They arrived at Hughenden, which only had a police station, maybe a few houses—I don't think if it would have even had a post office then. They then drove them on through Muttaburra and Aramac, all the way down to Adelaide.

It took them two years to take the sheep from 100 mile north of Charters Towers to Adelaide, droving. They shore them somewhere near Mitchell, and shore them again twelve months later as they followed down the Darling River. Down near Adelaide they punted them across the Murray River two hundred at a time and sold them all. They sold twenty thousand all up before they got to Adelaide. It's all written up in Hann's diary. That country north of Charters Towers just isn't sheep country.

Chapter 33

Conservation

DAD HAD ALWAYS built dams, because he didn't have the money to put down a bore. Artesian Bores started being put in in Australia during the 1890s; from around 1900 to 1920 there were boring plants all around the place. One of Dad's first jobs had been helping put down a bore at Redcliffe Station in 1912. It was the old percussion system—you had a heavy weight and thick steel, so heavy I couldn't even lift one end of the sinker bar. The end of it looked like a chisel and this used to go up and down all day worked with a rope on the surface 'pecking' at the soil; it dug into the dirt and you added water to it as you went. Because the weight was so heavy, it acted sort of like a magpie pecking. The water would turn the dirt into mud and then you'd pull that out; then you'd lower another pipe, say twenty foot long, with a valve on the end to trap the mud as it was pushed up the pipe as it was lowered, and you'd pull it up and remove another pipeful of mud. Most bores took months and months to put down, but they were an investment. You don't lose water to evaporation with tapped bores like you do with dams.

Back on Antrim, Lach and I had two flowing bores and we used to be able to pump water from a third. We put a new bore down at Antrim in 1958, when one of the other bores failed, and it took about eight months to dig. It was about 1800 feet deep. We got a good flow of water, about 70,000 gallons a day, which was more than we wanted. We put a big tap on it and put poly pipelines out to troughs where we wanted the water to go.

Some places put a bore at the top of a ridge and the bore drains flow free out along the ground like a spider's legs, with its centre being the bore. When they drill the bore, they have a head on it; it might initially squirt up and then settle down so you can put a tap on it. A tapped bore. That way it could be turned off, which made it easier for delving. But some didn't have a tap at all, not thinking that the Artesian Basin would drain away. Some of the bores had taps, but they were often left on with water running freely down the paddock. Only about 5 per cent of the water in a drain was used by stock and the rest ran out onto the ground, where a lot of it evaporated and the water was wasted. There were some bores around Cunnamulla pumping out a million gallons here and a million gallons there each day, and they were actually using less than 100 gallons of it. You're not allowed to irrigate out of bores, it was frowned upon by the water and irrigation government department, so that water was wasted.

I was keeping records of the levels in our bores and could see the water level was falling by a foot a year, so I moved in a UGA meeting that all bores be capped. I moved that all these flows be cut down, and that people should use poly pipe to get water to troughs, instead of letting the water flow out on the ground. It would be a costly process but I could see the benefits, better than having to dig deeper bores. God, they were going to hang, draw and quarter me, and I was told to never bring it up again.

At a following UGA meeting, other people had noticed the water levels were dropping and they were complaining about it because they were having to go deeper and deeper and having to pull more bores and it was costing more in manpower, equipment and casing. But a few of the laggards were still holding out, saying, 'I'm getting it for nothing—why should I spend money on it?' Lach and I were spouting to anyone who'd listen about the poly pipe. We put in the pipelines before the government brought in an act that said the old practice had to be changed—we knew it was going to come in, it had to come in.

Official conservation measures happened in the 1970s. After that, using poly pipes was supposed to be compulsory. They gave the landowners a couple of years, gave them an option to put in poly pipe on their bores and run them to where the water was needed; if they didn't put water conservation methods in place, the bore owners were told that bores would be closed down. Blow me down, one of the more critical blokes at that first UGA meeting, his son ended up getting a government job advising people and making them close their bores.

These days the water level in the Artesian Basin is starting to come back up again. Everybody is benefiting as the water is coming back.

Chapter 34

Limbri

ON 30 OCTOBER 1959, our second child, Julie Margaret, was born. And on the first of July 1960, Lach and I bought another property, Limbri, near Hughenden.

We bought Limbri from a bloke called William Allen, a well-known merino breeder. Limbri was one of several places owned by him and his father. Sir William Guildford Allen had been knighted for services to the Country Party; William junior and his family lived in Brisbane in Hamilton House, a mansion on a hill overlooking the Brisbane River.

Limbri was only 26 mile south-west of Hughenden, and it was 28,000 acres. Lach and I bought Limbri with our two wives, but we all still lived in the one house at Antrim 60 mile away. We'd begun paying our mortgage on Antrim almost twice as fast as we needed to—we wanted to get out of debt. We were shearing and fencing, and doing everything we could to pay the place off. But when Limbri came on the market, I went to our agents, Winchcombe Carson in Hughenden, who agreed to buy the sheep for us on account. I then went to Brisbane in the plane and saw the Bank of New South Wales, as they were (Westpac now), and secured an extension on our mortgage, so we bought Limbri.

Before this we had been selling three to four thousand lambs at Antrim. But when Lach and I bought Limbri the wether portion would come over to Limbri as lambs to grow out, mature, and the ewe lambs would stop at Antrim. As Limbri was on the railway line, I built a siding and sheep- and cattle-loading yards; we used to deal in sheep and cattle in good years, buying in young stock and growing them out. As it turned out, we could see the benefit of having one place, Antrim, to do the breeding on and one place to use as a wether growing-out block, and when we had the feed we could do a lot of dealing in sheep and cattle.

Limbri was badly rundown. It had just an old tin house that the manager and his family, the McNallys, had lived in, plus a fallen-down shearing shed. The water infrastructure was pretty rundown too. But we knew we could put in the work to turn it around.

The McNallys were a big family; there were five girls and one boy. They had a three-ton truck to go to town in—they wouldn't have fitted in an ordinary car. Mum and Dad sat up in the front, with all the kids in the back. The tin hut they lived in was in terrible shape. The tin came almost down to the ground, and there were no doors on

it when we went there, just hessian bags hanging in door-
ways. The toilet was a little bit of a landing that went out
from the house. There was a door on the toilet but none
on the shower, just a hessian bag between the toilet and
shower. The hut was virtually just two big rooms; because
there was a big family living there, they put a verandah all
around it and had big hessian bags hanging down to make
separate bedrooms along it.

We couldn't afford to keep the whole McNally family
on when we bought Limbri; at the time we hadn't finished
developing Antrim. We only needed one man at Limbri, so
we employed a bloke by the name of George Weatherhead
to help us run the place. I'd travel over to work with George
regularly, with fencing or working big mobs of stock.

Having a man on the place made it much easier than
working by yourself. It's fairly hopeless working by yourself if you're working cattle in a yard and mustering, it's
much easier having someone else there. Having George
there saved Lach having to come over. The rest of the time
George didn't have to do anything other than look after the
water and do any repairs. This suited him, and he lived in
that old hut for a few years.

About the same time as we bought Limbri, I was
approached by the local chap who represented our area
on the shire council to see if I was interested in going on
council. He was 100 mile out of town and wanted to get
out of politics, and on Antrim I was only 60 mile out. He
thought I was young and enthusiastic and they nominated

me. To be honest, I couldn't get on there quick enough, because I could see there was so much that needed to be done with the roads and in town.

I enjoyed being on council, really enjoyed it. I wasn't what you'd call a great speaker, but I used to put my point across fairly forcibly.

There were four divisions making up our country council, with the town being a separate fifth division, the town council. From these five areas were elected twelve councillors—three from the town and nine from the outlying divisions—and one chairman. I was never chairman, but I was the works chairman. The chairman used to go to local government meetings, but everybody wanted the roads and infrastructure done, so they used to come to me.

Flinders Shire Council was quite financial, but the Hughenden Town Council was broke when I first started. There were no bitumen streets; water and power were sporadic, because Council had to produce power with an old DC (direct current) generator that was run on diesel and would stop from time to time. The town's water supply came from bores and they had to get the water up with submersible electric pumps. So once the power went out, your water went out. There were no trees in the streets, because you couldn't water them. The town had virtually nothing. The council owned the cemetery, a rickety old dance hall and all the sporting infrastructure—tennis courts, a football field and a reasonable racecourse—but none of it was very well maintained.

There was an old undertaker, Mrs Monroe, who had taken over from her husband, Old Dan, when he passed away. She had this old-time hearse, must have been about a 1926 model Chevrolet with glass all the way round. She carried on there for a quite a few years after her husband died, but when she died, the council took that over as well.

When I started on council I really wanted to sort out water, reliable power, and trees in town.

The Flinders Shire Council was a big shire—18,000 square mile. Hughenden was roughly in the middle and of the council's boundaries which ran 100 mile north, 100 mile south, 70 miles east and 40 miles west of the town. The Flinders Highway, from Townsville to Mount Isa, ran through the middle, and the Hann Highway ran north to the Atherton Tablelands. Five artesian bores supplied water by submerged pumps, with a steel reservoir to hold about a day's water supply for Hughenden. There were seventy council stock-watering points in the shire that had to be maintained—about every ten mile you had a watering point. We also had hundreds of miles of shire and main roads to constantly look after.

I also maintained that if you wanted to have people come and live out there you had to supply amenities, and one of the things I wanted was good sporting facilities. I loved all sport, and as works chairman for the Flinders

Shire Council I was able to gain permission to hire council machinery out to different sporting groups—the racing club, football, cricket, golf, polocrosse and even the local showground—to improve their facilities at no cost. The only stipulation was that the men who used the machinery during the day must drive any machines used as they knew how to work them and the risk of damage wasn't so high. The sports clubs were responsible for the driver's wages, if necessary—usually a carton of 'lemonade'! It was a great idea and was much appreciated by all.

In those days everybody had a tennis court on their place. We had matches at our neighbours the McCarthys' place Moonby, almost a week about. Everybody took their own tucker and they boiled a billy, and it was a great turnout.

The north-west tennis tournament was the big tennis do out there, taking in competitors from all the towns—Hughenden, Winton and Mount Isa. A great friend, Roy Paine, and I used to compete—we were a bit unlucky once in the final, but we did eventually win the men's doubles. Tennis was big then; everyone played, and Australia had world-class champions like Rod Laver, Margaret Court and Roy Emerson. All the kids wanted to be like them. It's not so popular in Australia now, but I still love a game of tennis.

Back then there were quite a few people living on the different properties, and the area was very active socially. All the big places would have had one or two jackaroos working on them, and the really big places had maybe six or eight jackaroos, as well as cooks, fencers and contractors. If the families had children, there would also be governesses, who created a lot of interest—a lot of marriages came out of governesses and jackaroos meeting on stations. When we were on Antrim, Lach and I had two jackaroos as well as ourselves, and we had George on at Limbri. In the 1960s, every weekend without fail—unless it was raining—there was something on within 30 mile of you on someone's property.

It's really sad out there now, there's not much social life anymore; you virtually have to travel into town to socialise. There's just one man out at Antrim now, and some of the adjoining properties are now run from one place, so the old homesteads are locked up and empty. Back then even the smaller places, running, say, eight thousand sheep, always had a man, but you can't afford to employ them anymore.

As well as tennis courts, some of the places had cricket pitches. Some also had clay pigeon traps, which became popular, but it could be an expensive sport. There was still a lot of money around as wool prices were quite good—not the same as during the wool boom, but not as low as they are now—and a lot of us used to shoot in our area. There would have been a dozen trap sheds all around us.

To build a trap, you used a big water tank with one section cut out, and you'd build up a mound on either side of it with the cut-out section in the direction you wanted to fire out of. You'd have what they call a 'trap', a mechanism to shoot out these 'clay pigeons', which were shaped just like a saucer and about the same size, black and made of clay. The clay pigeons themselves were very expensive; but then, after you got good at it, you could make quite a bit of money out of it at competitions. Quite a few blokes, when they got good at clay pigeon shooting, would travel to Townsville or Sydney or wherever and compete in clay trap competitions, but I only ever competed locally. I won one local trap-shoot competition and came away with a beautiful shotgun, which I had for many years, but then I had to watch it being destroyed by the police in the gun amnesty after the 1996 Port Arthur massacre in Tasmania.

One time I had to go to Townsville for three days on council business. My sister Ethel and her husband, David, were looking at getting a Cessna 172, and she wanted to get her licence as well. When Ethel found out I was going to be there for a few days, she said to me, 'I'm coming with you, and I can get six hours' tuition in the plane in Townsville with an instructor.'

We drove the 300 mile from Hughenden and stayed at the Queens Hotel. There were still no motels, as I mentioned before—they were just building one in Townsville at the time, but everyone still stayed in big hotels. This Queens Hotel was *the* place to stay. It was a beautiful big place— two storeys right on the seafront. Everybody stopped there; it was the social hub of Townsville.

We got there at eleven o'clock at night, and signed in as Mrs Hardy and Mr Tindall. The porter took Ethel upstairs and right down one end of the hall, close on 100 yards from the office. Back he came for me, and we went along the bottom floor, about 100 yards in the opposite direction. I got to my room, showered and got ready for bed and then thought, 'I haven't talked to Ethel about tomorrow.' With flying you usually start at daylight or early in the morning, to avoid the thermals, and I knew I'd have to remind her about getting up early. I was in just a pair of shorty pyjamas, but there was no one around, so up the stairs I go. I was just going into her room when this porter came along, saw me opening Ethel's door and started giggling knowingly. And I thought, 'Oh yeah, fair enough.' I knew Ethel wouldn't wake up at daylight, so I told her I'd be back then and made my way back down to my room for the night.

Early the next morning, up the stairs I went and woke her. I was coming back out of her room in the pre-dawn and the same porter came along and saw me, and he chuckled to himself as we walked past each other. That was alright; I just ignored him really. But from then on, the staff had us marked. In the great big dining room where we had our meals, we could be the first in there and they'd serve us last. I thought I saw some of them pointing at us as we sat there waiting to be served.

There was this old girl in the office—she'd been there a hundred years—and when I went to check out, I told her that Mrs Hardy would also be checking out shortly. She was very put out with the thought of an unmarried couple being together in her establishment. I thought, 'Bugger yer,' and said, 'We're travelling together, you know!'

When I came home and told Barb that story, she wouldn't stop there anymore—she was worried that this old girl would make some comment that I was in with my wife this time! I knew what they were thinking; that's just how it was.

When we bought our brand-new Holden after the strike, I hadn't paid much attention to the number plate until it was pointed out to me that the registration prefix was PEE. All the Queensland registration prefixes started with P at the time. One day in a council meeting one of the councillors stood up to say something and then became distracted when he looked out the great big glass doors onto the parking lot. He said to us, 'Just have a look out there at those cars.' We looked out and saw a line-up of almost the same Holden vehicles. When we looked back at him blankly, he said, 'Look at the rego plates.' Mine was parked beside the chairman's Holden and its plate had the prefix POO; the shire clerk's vehicle had POX; another bloke's rego plate started with PIS.

It was a bit of a joke from then on, although we seriously wondered if the bloke who worked in the Main Roads office, where they were distributing the Queensland number plates, reckoned we were such a shitty council that we deserved those plates. I don't know—there would have been hundreds of cars with similar prefixes, but it so happened that four of us were on council in the same town. The shire clerk eventually bought his council car for his daughter, but she wouldn't drive it until the plates were changed.

Chapter 35

A bad year

SOME SAY BAD luck comes in threes; well, it came in fives in 1964.

Barb was pregnant with our third child when she got hepatitis. We were driving back through Dalby and we pulled up at night at a café, because Maree wanted to go to the toilet. When they came back, Barb said to me, 'That toilet is a stinking horrible mess.'

I think it was ten days later—it was exactly the right time for hepatitis to show itself—when she became very crook, and she was sick for quite a while. She moved to her parents' place to recuperate, taking nearly five-year-old Julie with her. Maree stayed with me at Antrim; at the time, she was in first grade and was being schooled by a governess at Marg and Lach's new house with their little boy, Robert.

The weather was fairly dry. We had a flowing bore on Antrim, and it used to supply the house, woolshed and a whole lot of paddocks, but then it just suddenly stopped flowing. The bore had caved in; unbeknown to us, it hadn't been cased all the way to the bottom when it was originally put down, so after a while, within 200 feet of the top, it rotted away and the dirt fell in. Some days it would start to flow again, but it was no longer reliable, so we decided to put another one down beside it.

We got in some contractors—people who had their own boring plant. But good bore contractors were very rare, just like good fencing contractors—they had to know what they were doing, and they couldn't afford to make a mistake. If part of the drill rod broke off right there and they couldn't get it out, they would have to start all over again. That happened to a friend of ours with his boring contractor.

It cost us £62,000 to renew—an absolute fortune—but we couldn't live without the water, and neither could the animals. The contractors went down to 2675 feet and, when they left, it still wasn't working. They hadn't reached the Artesian Basin, but we still had to pay them. They came back a few months later and worked on the bore and went down deeper; it all came good and the bore came back to flowing about 50,000 gallons a day—we had plenty of water then. But it cost a lot of money.

While the contractor was still working on the new bore, a big flash flood came through Antrim and we lost nearly all our sheep—about two thousand ewes, twenty-two hundred wethers and four thousand lambs. The catchment received over twelve inches of rain in one night—we normally had only ten inches of rain on the place in a year. All the heavy rain had fallen in the catchment just up the creek, and down it came. You can't insure against floods like that. All of the new ringlock fencing we'd just put up, we lost in one night. It wasn't just the floodgates that went, which were the usual problem in floods, it was entire fences; the water went right out for miles and ran fast, taking everything with it. When the water eventually went back down, in one place we found a sheep hanging on the eight-foot-high telephone wire; it had never flooded that high in living memory.

Then, while trying to find and muster any remaining sheep, I had a bad horseriding accident off this mongrel horse. We didn't have any fences left, so we got a young chap from town to come out and give us a hand with mustering. He didn't like the saddle he was on—it was quite old and hadn't been used for a while—so I told him to take mine. He had such a nice quiet old horse, he was flat out getting him to shift. But this horse I was on was so wild—he was a young horse that could really buck, a real exhibitionist. What happened exactly I don't know, but he went down into the creek at full gallop and the saddle slipped and both the girth and the surcingle broke, and I was speared straight into the side of the bank. I broke my shoulder blade, a bone in my neck, a bone in my elbow and four ribs, and tore my diaphragm, which let my gut into my chest cavity.

The horse went home without a saddle or rider, and Lach tracked him back and found me unconscious at the bottom of the creek. I was lucky in a way—there was quite a bit of water still in the creek and I had landed just short of it. If I'd landed in the water unconscious, I wouldn't be here today. They got the ambulance out from town, and I was laid up then for a month. I don't know what was worse, the broken shoulder blade or the broken ribs; but anyway, as long as I didn't cough, I was right. I was back in the lamb marking yards in a month, and shearing was coming up. I had to get back to work.

Marg had been looking after Maree; when I came out of hospital, Maree and I moved back into the old house on Antrim. It was a tremendous big place. Back in 1910, when the house was built, they would have had a maid and a cook, as well as the household. Barb, the kids and I still lived in the old kitchen block, and the old homestead was empty because Marg and Lach had moved into their new house.

We used to get butter from town; the store would wrap it in wet bags cut from old Jute sacks and send it out with the mail and with boxes of other supplies. I came home late one night in the middle of shearing, picked Maree up from Marg's, put her to bed and realised the old Rayburn stove needed cleaning out. I cleaned the ashes into a drum; then, rather than go out and empty it in the dark, I put it under the main house, close to where we had those butter bags and empty boxes stored. I must have dropped a coal in the dark; it smouldered through the night, and the butter bags and boxes eventually caught fire. Luckily I woke to the smell of smoke; when I opened my eyes, I could see a bit of a flickering glow coming out of the old house. I managed to get myself and Maree out, but she was worried about her budgerigar and guinea pig, so I went back into the kitchen block and grabbed them out. But that's all we got.

By the time I was out a second time, the fire had spread across the passageway and into the kitchen block where we'd been sleeping. It was so quick. We lost everything—well, nearly everything. I saved Maree's pets, but we lost all of our station books, our wedding presents, clothes and photos—all sort of bits and pieces. Once the fire got into the inside of the house, it just exploded.

There I was standing in a pair of shorty pyjamas and a pair of boots I'd managed to pull on as I went out, and Maree was in her pyjamas holding her precious pets. The shearers rushed over from the nearby quarters to see if they could help, as did Lach from his house. But there was nothing any of us could do except watch it burn.

Maree had ridden Julie's three-wheeled metal tricycle to Marg and Lach's the day before, so that was saved, but we had precious little else. We didn't even have a toothbrush. We had no insurance, so we had to start from scratch.

I had to ring Barb at her parents' and tell her the house was gone, which was pretty tough. She and Julie just had the clothes they'd taken with them. It was my fault, cleaning out the coals after a big day in the shed, and I must have been careless. So we lost our home.

*

From a very young age our two girls just loved their guinea pigs. When we were travelling anywhere, the guineas came too. We had sold our car in Longreach the previous year and were going to Brisbane by Greyhound bus, intending to get a new one. A lady sitting in front of us was eating an apple, so I asked her if I could have the core. This lady looked at me as if I had just crawled out from under a rock, but gave it to me all the same. Our girls were sitting behind us, with the guineas well hidden, and I handed the core over to them; when the guineas smelt the apple, they started to squeal. Apparently it was not in the bus regulations for the girls to have 'livestock' in the coach, but the driver said he didn't hear or see a thing.

After our home burnt down, Maree and I moved into the shearers' quarters when shearing had finished. There was no electricity at the quarters, so we were relying once again on carbide lights. We had a drop toilet down on the flat—it wasn't allowed to be near the quarters for health reasons—and we'd sometimes get little surprises.

The toilet was placed over a concrete drainage pipe, which was about two foot six in diameter and had a ten-foot drop. The snakes would crawl into the loo looking for shade, and often fall into the pit and couldn't get out. So I rigged up a snake catcher. I'd drop a rope with a noose on the end of it down through a long poly pipe; I'd point the rope towards the snake, drop the noose over its head, tighten it and gently pull the snake into the pipe, so it couldn't bite me when I lifted it out.

I would bag them and send them off to Ram Chandra, an Indian bloke who lived near Mackay and was a snake showman and who was experimenting with milking snakes to develop antivenins to give to people bitten by various snakes. Years before, the Commonwealth Serum Laboratories (CSL) had considered him a bit of an amateur and wouldn't accept the venom he collected, which stirred the Queenslanders who supported him into action. Everyone lobbied the government on his behalf, and CSL eventually accepted venom from him and developed the antivenin for the taipan snake.

Barb went into labour not long after we lost the house. Our third daughter, Tracey, was born alive, but died the next day. As well as Barb having hepatitis through most of the pregnancy, apparently one of the problems with Tracey was that the cord had been wrapped tightly around her neck for too long. The doctor told me that had she survived she could have been a 'problem child'; he wasn't too distraught about it I suppose is one way to put it. We have often thought that with a better doctor she might have had a chance.

I saw Tracey quite a few times, but Barb never saw her— the mothers didn't in those days. Barb often cries today about the fact she never saw her. She was such a skinny little thing because she just wasn't getting the blood supply as she developed. Poor little dear.

Nineteen sixty-four was a bad year.

Chapter 36

Change

THE FOLLOWING YEAR I was driving along the road between Hughenden and Winton when I saw these two blokes on the side of the road. It was only a dirt track then, and it was 140 mile (225 kilometres) between the two towns. These two blokes were driving a Toyota four-wheel drive; they asked me for directions, asking where the cattle were and where the sheep were. So I asked what they were doing, and they told me they were releasing dung beetles. I had never heard of them.

The CSIRO (Commonwealth Scientific and Industrial Research Organisation) brought dung beetles out from South Africa in the 1960s, and to my knowledge there are about five different types. As far as I know, they never told anybody what they were doing, but I asked all about it.

The dung beetle is wonderful around cattle, cleaning up their dung very effectively. Some dung beetles eat the whole lot of the dung, getting in underneath it and leaving a thin crust; some of them roll it into a ball and tunnel it into the earth and live or breed on it, effectively removing it from the surface and away from the flies. They are completely different, and they are all wonderful. They are also good at cleaning up any offal or dead animals. If you leave a kangaroo or sheep carcass, they'll eat all of it in a day or two until there is nothing left. We used to kill our own meat, and when you let out the paunch or the gut you'd have a wheelbarrowful of yuck to dispose of. But when the dung beetles were in full flight, if you dropped all of the guts out on the ground, the next day it would be a damp patch about four feet across—they would have either eaten or buried the whole lot.

They eat anything. Sometimes you go to pick up a dead sheep and there is just wool, with nothing underneath it, just bones. So then flies couldn't breed in it. It was absolutely tremendous. About three years after they officially let the dung beetles go, it just about eliminated bung eyes from sandy blight and other sores caused by flies.

You can always tell a dung beetle. If you hold them in your hand, you'll feel them trying to squeeze between your fingers as they try to burrow out. Driving at night, the bigger dung beetles would hit the windscreen and make a clicking noise, but you rarely see them in the day.

The dung beetle is one of the best things brought out to Australia, unlike the cane toad. The cane toad was introduced to Queensland in 1935 from Hawaii to eat the cane beetle, which was destroying sugar cane crops. They ate the beetles, but they also poisoned native snakes, goannas and insects and contaminated water, and were just a disaster.

After living in the shearers' quarters at Antrim for about a year, we decided to move to Limbri. George moved to another job and we lived in the old tin hut for about eighteen months before we built a place up on a high ridge, so you could see everywhere. You could see the trains leaving Hughenden 26 mile out. You could see them coming nearly the whole way, and then they'd disappear as they went down into Walkers Creek, and you'd see them come back out again. It was a great spot.

Mum died in 1966. Dad was devastated, but he eventually married again. He wore out two wives—he wore the second one out too, and they were both younger than he was. After Mum died, he left a manager on at MacFarlane Downs and bought a house in Toowoomba, where he met his second wife, Stella; I think he met her through a relative. They'd come out to MacFarlane for a couple of months in the wintertime and go around the boundaries. He always had to go around the boundaries—why I wouldn't know—and Stella had to open all the gates. She died a couple of years before Dad.

Dad achieved a lot in his lifetime. He was one of the first out there, and he started with nothing. He had to work hard for everything. He died thirteen years after Mum.

Ethel's husband, David Hardy, died in about 1968, just two years after Mum, leaving Ethel with two boys and a little girl. What happened was, he was flying about in his plane looking for eaglehawks that were taking the lambs. When you fly over a hill—especially any of those hills with steep cliffs surrounding them, the cliffs are probably anything from five to twenty foot all around it and flat on top. The wind goes over one side and sucks down the other side, following the contour of the hill. He was heading up a hill and into the wind; he was going alright, but when he got to the top of the hill, this wind just pulled him straight down so he hit the cliff on the side of the hill. Ethel took her kids to school in Toowoomba and eventually met and married widower Colin Clift, whose kids were at the same school. They still live in Toowoomba and David and Ethel's eldest child John now runs Verastone.

Chapter 37

Educating bush kids

EDUCATION IS ONE of the toughest aspects of living in the bush. Floods, fires and droughts come and go, but the kids still have to be educated. There are a lot of wonderful governesses, but eventually the children must go to boarding school for the last few years or move into town, and the family is split up for probably the best years of family life. It is terribly costly to the family emotionally, but also financially, with travel fares and boarding fees.

When we moved to Limbri we advertised in the Brisbane *Courier-Mail* for a governess to teach Maree and Julie. We used the old correspondence system, similar to what we'd had out at Beatrice as kids. The lessons were sent back to Brisbane and returned marked, but more regularly than in our day. We had a separate schoolroom in a building outside of the house, so the girls weren't distracted by the phone ringing and people and activities coming and going in the house. But they'd still look out the window and say, 'Oh, Dad's coming in with a mob of sheep. I wonder what he's going to do with them,' or something like that. Anything to get out of doing schoolwork.

Maree on her pony 'MacFarlane Gay', helping Hugh move ewes and lambs.

Our kids were involved with everything on the station, or wanted to be. One time when Julie was about five years old, we had a couple of hundred head of bullocks to sell. The agent came out with a buyer to look at them, and there was a big old fat bull there as well. We'd just put them into the yard and Julie was walking along between the agent and buyer. She pointed out the bull to them and this silly bugger said, 'How do you know it's a bull?' So Julie told him all about bulls and cows and calves.

We never hid anything from the kids. They were always round the animals. Our girls knew all about the bulls and why you take them out at certain times, and why the rams are only in the paddock for eight weeks. They saw bulls riding cows, and lambs and calves being born; they saw animals die. Telling fairy stories just doesn't work. So she really got into him and he looked at the agent and said, 'Well, ask a silly question . . .'

As the kids got older, they wanted a stallion to breed ponies. Dad still loved his horses, and in 1953, when he and Mum were starting to get grandchildren, he had decided to import and breed some Welsh mountain ponies for them. He wanted his grandkids to love horses as much as he did. By then Arthur and Eva had two boys and a girl; Godfrey had married a local girl, Kath, in 1952 and they were expecting a baby; and Lach and Marg were just married. So Dad brought out four mares and a stallion from Daisy Broderick, founder of the Coed Coch Stud in North Wales. Miss Broderick had been recommended as having the best Welsh mountain ponies in all of the United Kingdom; her ponies had won champion of the British Isles a couple of times. Dad and Miss Broderick corresponded for many years after he imported the ponies. He wrote to her and told her about them—how many were born and how they were going.

One of the mares that Dad imported bumped her head unloading in Sydney and died, but the others made their way to MacFarlane Downs and bred some lovely little ponies. The colt he imported was called Coed Coch Pilan and was by one of Miss Broderick's champion stallions, Tregoyd Starlight. A lot of people brought mares to Pilan because the progeny were so quiet, and they made terrific kids' ponies. Even though they were often smaller than a lot of people were used to, they still bought the ponies from Dad. Or they brought their bigger mares to his stallion, and then they would usually get a bigger foal anyway, halfway between the mare and stallion in size.

Dad bred quite a few ponies for the grandkids over the years—he tried to give them a filly each—and when our girls wanted to breed their own, Dad helped them find a suitable young colt. The girls bred some nice little ponies over time with their mares.

Governesses stayed with us at Limbri, and it was quite an experience for them. They were all great girls. We had three governesses all up for the girls before they went away to high school.

Each governess stayed about twelve months after they had finished school, a bit like the 'gap year' kids do now. The first was a Brisbane girl, Beverley Beaumont. She was a city girl who wanted to experience the west and get an insight into life in the bush. We told her what the accommodation was like in the tin hut at Limbri; when she first started, we spoke with her father and said what the set-up was—that we'd just lost our house in a fire and were moving into a place with just a tin shed for a home, and that we were building a new home. Although Barbara didn't meet him through us, she ended up marrying our doctor, Bruce Stringer.

Bruce was the first bloke ever to be saved from a taipan bite. He'd been bitten by the snake in his schoolyard in Cairns when he was about ten, and the medical staff said he never had a chance, but the hospital got onto Ram Chandra, who had been experimenting with antivenin. He said it had never been used on a human before, but they could try it. Bruce was the first bloke they used it on, and he survived, although he still has a great big scar on his leg where he was bitten.

After Beverley left us, she did her nursing training at the Princess Alexandra (PA) Hospital in Brisbane, and that's where she met Bruce. He was doing his internship at the PA, and they eventually got married. They went overseas for twelve months, then came back and he took the GP job at Hughenden and we reconnected.

Years later, Beverley and Bruce would come out to our place to socialise—play tennis, go pig or roo shooting. At the time I used to organise controlled mating for the heifers who were first-time mothers—I'd put the bulls in with them for ten days, a fortnight, no longer, so the calves would all be born around the same time. I was running about thirty heifers, and when they were due to calve I'd bring them in close to the house so I could watch them. One morning when Bev and Bruce were visiting, the heifers had started calving, and Bev said, 'I've never seen a calf born.' I told her she'd see one born that day. In the paddock we came across a heifer with just the front hooves starting to poke out, so I said we should leave her for three or four hours and come back after lunch.

We went back out and she was still in the same position, the birth hadn't progressed, and I said, 'We've gotta help her out.' We had a little Mini Moke at the time and I said to Bruce, 'She's a big strong heifer, but we need to give her a hand.' I told him to get in and drive the Moke. We came alongside her and I grabbed her tail, got up to her head and pulled her down so she was lying on her side. She was pretty tired from being in labour for so long, so she wasn't objecting much. I tied the heifer's front hooves together and checked the calf was in the right position. The calf's head was between his front legs and he was ready to come out, but he was firmly stuck. He wasn't coming out by himself; she needed a bit more help.

I tied baling twine above the front hooves of the emerging calf. You need to pull the calf slightly downwards, never straight out, so we pulled the Moke up behind her and I tied the baling twine onto the Moke's front bumper bar. I told Bruce to slowly reverse on my signal while I put pressure on the twine in a downwards motion, and we eased the calf out with each contraction and saved both the calf and the heifer.

Anyway, a few days later there was a lady in Hughenden having a baby and they were having a bit of trouble; Bruce told me later he wanted to ask the matron to ring me and tell me to bring in the Moke and those two bits of baling twine. It became a bit of a joke between us. We still keep in touch with them; they live in Geelong now. Bruce and Beverley are a lovely couple.

The last governess we had was Cathy Crittenden, who came from the Glasshouse Mountains north of Brisbane, and she married a carpenter she met when he was working on our house on Limbri.

After a few years of correspondence schooling with governesses, Barb organised private board for Maree and Julie in Hughenden with a wonderful older couple, Hector and Mavis Alloway. We thought the girls would benefit from being able to live in someone's home, that it was a good first step before going away to boarding school. Julie was about eight, I think, when she went to the Alloways', and Maree was eleven. They would come back home every weekend.

Maree went to boarding school at St Anne's school in Townsville for her last three years of school and hated every day of it. Julie only had one year away at boarding school in Brisbane, which she enjoyed. Julie stayed with the Alloways for longer than Maree, and used to go shopping and do things with Mavis all the time, so much so that some people thought her name was Julie Alloway.

Barb never attempted to teach the kids except once,

when we couldn't get a governess for a few weeks and school had started. But they didn't take any notice of her. Nowadays kids out there have got School of the Air, where they have correspondence lessons with a teacher via the wireless. Each western area has their region for distance education and the south-western region is now based out of Charleville.

School of the Air can have its moments. Our grandson was out at Boulia in Far Western Queensland with Maree and her husband a few years back, and I think every Monday morning they have a session on School of the Air for the kids to talk about what they did on the weekend. A bit like Show and Tell—'We went fishing,' or 'We went to a party,' or whatever they did.

Our grandson was listening in while the teacher was talking to one little boy. She asked him, 'How was your weekend, Johnny?'

'Not too good, Miss.'

'Why, what happened?' the teacher asked.

'Me and me dad went mustering. We had all these cattle drafted, and we spent two whole days drafting.'

'What happened then? That would have been fun, Johnny.'

'Aw no, Miss. Dad sent me down to open a gate and I opened the wrong gate and they all got boxed up together again. Dad went crook and called me a "fuckin idiot".'

Of course the teacher was a bit flustered and said, 'Well, I think that's enough, Johnny,' and went on to the next one.

Maree was listening in too, and she didn't know what to do when she heard him come out with that—she didn't know whether to cover her boy's ears or what to do. School of the Air, like any school I suppose, it can have its unpredictable moments.

Chapter 38

Council business

IN 1969 WE employed John Lucas on Limbri. John was a
great bloke, very quiet, very honest, and he married a girl
who had been born and raised on Limbri, Eileen McNally.
They moved into the tin hut, to which we'd had a bit of
work done, and we moved into our new home on the ridge.

Limbri was everything to the McNallys—the kids had
all grown up there, and Eileen loved being back on the
place. They were with us for a few years from May 1969;
they then moved into town to educate their kids. You might
have a wonderful couple working on your place, but then
they start a family, and they either have to move to town
for the children's education or send them away to boarding
school. But still the bush is loved by the people that live
there, and you become self-sufficient. I suppose I feel sorry
for people in the cities that go day to day, year to year doing
the same thing all their lives.

Employing John meant I could spend more time on jobs for the council around the district. Being on council was rewarding and at times humorous. One time I had to go down to Brisbane for a local government meeting. At Limbri we had one of those old washing machines with the rollers on top; it was so old that the gearbox had gone on it. I thought I'd take the part down to Brisbane with me and get a replacement part while I was there. I looked up where I could find the parts and the address was in Mary Street, in the heart of Brisbane, not far from where the meeting was.

I hadn't realised, but Mary Street and nearby Charlotte Street were the brothel streets. When I got there I couldn't see any building that looked like it sold washing machine parts, so I stopped a bloke and said, 'I'm looking for this place,' and showed him the address. He said, 'That's it, that buck-coloured building over there.' Well, I didn't want to tell him I was colour blind, but I reckoned I could work out which one it was from where he was pointing.

This was about half past nine or ten in the morning, and I walked over, walked straight in to the building, and there was about six to ten girls sitting around in the front room. I walked in and one of them came up to greet me and said, 'You're here early, dear,' and we just stood there chatting, and she was a lovely girl. And then another girl came over and said, 'Can I help you?' By then I'd woken up well and truly to where I was, and I said, 'Look, what you're selling I'm not after, and what I'm after you haven't got,' as a joke. And we laughed as we stood there, a bit awkwardly.

Then I said goodbye and went to walk out. But I knew it wasn't far from where the meeting was to be held, and I thought, 'If one of these bushie blokes sees me coming out of a brothel at ten in the morning, I'll never hear the end of it.' So I looked out carefully, peeked left and right, then shot out and took off. I probably looked even more guilty than I would have otherwise, but I made it to the meeting—needless to say, without the washing machine part.

Queensland Rail needed tons of sand and basalt for a line upgrade, and the Flinders River, which ran through the town of Hughenden, was a convenient supply. I found a bloke out there on the Flinders who had had a business crushing basalt, but he had gone broke. He had this big crushing plant on the river and there was 10,000 cubic yards (7650 cubic metres) of gravel that had already been pulled out of the river. I got a bloke who knew a bit about it to look over everything, and because it was quite a bad time financially out there the council purchased both the plant and gravel at a good price.

We put four of our men out there to work on this crushing plant, and we didn't even have to sieve it, the crushed stone was perfect for us to use maintaining the roads, and to sell onto Queensland Rail. The council made a heap of money out of this crusher and eventually sold it on to the railway and main roads authorities. Things like that I just loved organising and seeing work.

We got electricity on in 1966, and that was really something. The regional electricity board came to the council in the mid-sixties and said they could link the town to the power grid, which meant being able to reliably pump water into the town. Council could put in AC (alternating current) power—this is the type of electricity most commonly used in homes and is extremely versatile, because its voltage can be changed through a transformer. DC or direct current power was the first type of electricity to be commercially transmitted—the electrical current travels through a circuit in only one direction, like battery power, and that was what the council used for its generators prior to putting in AC.

I wasn't on the council power board, but when they came out to put the power on in town, I still asked, 'When are you going to give us rural power?' and they asked, 'When do you want it?' and I answered, 'Yesterday!'

The engineer and architect from the power company were left with me for a day, and we sat down then and there and worked out a plan. We sketched out a wagon wheel shape from Hughenden with all of these spur lines out to the whole shire. The men from the power company had to go away and do a costing and get back to us, and in the meantime I got the graziers together and we organised one representative on each spur, someone to organise each line. When they gave us a total costing, we worked out that each property was only up for about two hundred pounds, and for that they would be guaranteed an electricity line. It used to cost us that much a year just for coke for our stoves, so we couldn't get it on quick enough.

Getting the power on was one of the best things I helped organise while on council. We got power on just about before anybody else in the west of Queensland. It was the greatest thing to ever happen in that western area in so many ways. Before then we only had kerosene fridges and you couldn't leave a kerosene fridge going all the time, so you couldn't have much fresh meat, vegies or milk, especially in summer. It was wonderful; not only did we get power, we then had unlimited water in town from the bores, all of the time.

Chapter 39

April Fool

It was April Fools' Day 1969 when a bloke came up from Hillston, two hundred mile south of Nyngan in New South Wales, and I sold him a hundred and forty head of cattle, four thousand weaner lambs, nine thousand head of sheep all up including the lambs. I just about emptied Limbri with that sale—all we had left was a bull and an old cow, and two or three horses.

As I've said, floods and drought were commonplace out there. The thing with drought is you get time to think about it. In a flood you don't; you may be lucky enough to get some warning, maybe a week to ten days in the channel country, but nothing if it's a flash flood. In a drought, though, you can usually reduce numbers before it gets really bad. We hadn't had much rain by 1 April that year, which was my cut-off day. In that downs country, if you hadn't had rain through the wet season, from December to March, you've had it, and you want to get your animals out.

This bloke originally came to buy two thousand sheep. I took him out to the bore where the five paddocks all came in together and he saw all of our stock—over nine thousand sheep and one hundred and forty cattle. He offered to buy the lot and I agreed.

Everyone was telling me, 'Oh, you're mad. What's got into you?' But I said, 'Look, if it doesn't rain I'm going to be lucky, and if it does rain I'm going to be stupid.' But in 1969 it didn't rain.

If you sell a mob like that and it does rain, you may pay a bit more to replace them. But so what—it's better than taking a huge loss by selling when you and everyone else absolutely has to or, worse, losing the sheep in drought. There is nothing worse than a bad smell in your paddock. Rather than taking the risk in that country, I decided to sell. The thing is, out there it doesn't pay to buy feed for your stock, because you don't know when the drought is going to end; if it goes on for two years, you're broke. So the first of April, April Fools' Day, is when I decide if I'll sell, and most can decide whether I'm a fool or not.

We still had another fifteen thousand breeding ewes on Antrim, and after the sale we brought three thousand ewes over to Limbri; we lightened them up and spread them out on the two places, and we didn't have any losses at all. It didn't rain until the December and then we had good feed and could support more animals again. The country around Isisford still hadn't had any rain by then and it was still droughted out, so I went down and bought three thousand wethers, full wool at half the price. We saved our own and bought back into more sheep when we had the feed.

If you get a bad drought year you have to sell or go droving to keep the animals alive, and it can be followed by another drought year. It really is the land of droughts and flooding rain.

Chapter 40

Plane, train and automobile

IN JUST OVER a week in February 1970, I saw three separate accidents, with a bus, a plane and a train.

I was travelling along behind a bus one day out on our gravel road when it tipped over in front of me. The front wheel sort of went into a table drain on the side of the road that was filled with water after a storm; the bus sank into it and then slowly tipped over onto its side. There were only about fifteen people in the bus and nobody was hurt—there might have been a couple of people with skin off and a few bruises, but everyone was able to get out. I had a big steel rope with me and I hooked it onto the pillar on the bus's windscreen and pulled it back onto its wheels. The passengers hopped back in and away they went.

A few days later, I was driving straight towards the railway line from home. I saw the train coming and then this great cloud of dust went up and I thought, 'What the deuce is going on?' Only the engine came out of the dust, with no carriages behind it. The ballast trucks following the engine just broke away—one of the big connecting shackles broke, I think. The front truck derailed and the trucks following were jumping one on top of another. Some of them went ten to fifteen feet up into the air out of the dust.

It was quite a spectacle to witness. The driver eventually pulled the engine up and looked back in disbelief, completely unhurt. I did well out of it in the end, because I wanted some loads of sand and it was carrying mostly sand and gravel for ballast. I just helped myself to what was left behind after the cleanup.

The plane crash happened, about twenty mile from us, and I was one of the first ones to arrive, before the police. I forget what type of plane it was, but I know my brother Lach went for a fly in it when it first came out there. It was a lovely-looking plane, and my brother and another pilot and neighbour Wally Schultz had taken off from the Hughenden strip. When they brought it back, they said they wouldn't get in it again. It was good in a cold climate, but no good out in the west—not enough lift.

At the time of the accident, there were two men and two teenage daughters of one of the blokes in the plane. One of the girls was seventeen or eighteen, and the other about sixteen. These two chaps had flown into a neighbour's place in the middle of the day to have a look at some sheep. The plane was overloaded; the plane was full of petrol and four people, and the strip wasn't very good.

As they were trying to take off on the runway, the wing of the plane hit a tree and the wing was ripped off. The plane dived straight into a creekbed about six or eight foot deep running alongside the airstrip, and then it burst into flames. The fuel tanks were full and caught alight, and it all just burnt there. When I arrived, I had to use a firefighter I had in my ute to put the bodies out. The pilot had been thrown out in front of the plane and was still alight, but his three passengers were still in the burning plane. It was horrible.

The council undertaker was away, so the council sent out two mechanics from the depot in a truck with four coffins on the back; but they took one look and they wouldn't come near it. The local sergeant of police came out and told us we had to wait for the doctor to come and pronounce the people dead. He then took one look at it and said, 'Oh Hugh, you can handle this,' and left, saying he had other jobs to do.

The accident had happened right on the tick of one o'clock and the doctor couldn't come out immediately, because he was operating. He arrived at sundown to pronounce them dead; then I had to start putting them in the boxes, by myself. The council blokes wouldn't have anything to do with it and waited in the truck under a tree.

I knew who the people were, and I'd seen the girls a month or so before—they were very attractive girls—but I didn't know them well; I guess that made it a little easier. It's just one of those things you do in the bush, I suppose.

Never thought about it at the time, but the more I thought about it afterwards, the more crook I was at this police sergeant—I thought it was his job, not mine.

The plane crash was the worst of the three. After all of that, Barb and I decided to get away for a while.

Chapter 41

Sochi and the Kanebo Mill

SOME FRIENDS DOWN the way from us had been to Japan and visited the mills that bought our wool. The Japan World Expo was also on in Osaka in 1970 and we thought it would be interesting to have a look at. I had an insurance policy that I could cash, and Barb and I thought, 'We'll go to Japan and spend the money on that.' You didn't fly overseas much in those days; we went on a ship. It had eighty passengers, but it wasn't a cruise ship—it had mostly cargo.

We were out in the middle of the Pacific, both of us sitting on the deck, and I turned to Barb and said, 'I can smell wool.' Barb looked at me as if I was mad, but I insisted, 'I can!' She told me that it must have been on my clothes or hands or something. When we docked, we saw them unloading bales of wool. It had been in the cargo hold below deck, so I wasn't mad after all.

Coming into Yokohama on the boat, we were only

half an hour out and still couldn't see land—all we could see was a brown fog on the horizon, and it was like that right into the harbour. We couldn't work out what it was and we asked some of the crew on the boat, and they said, 'It's smog.' Smog was unheard of in Australia then. It was dreadful in both Tokyo and Osaka, and it was hot too—it was their summer.

We went on the bullet train, which travelled at 120 miles per hour, to Osaka for the Expo. It was a real experience, a world fair showcasing countries from around the world. Most of the Japanese were hoping tourists would come, which they did, and they left going themselves until the last few days. Three hundred thousand people were there with us on the last day. It was the most people I'd ever seen in my life. We were walking down this great big avenue; I'm not very tall, but I was a head taller than most Japanese and you could see a black crawling mass of heads—no one was wearing any hats, and it looked like a blanket waving in the wind as everyone walked along.

One of the agents who sold our wool knew a Japanese buyer, Sochi Hiramatsu, and he invited me to come and visit their mill. The mill was one of the biggest in Japan at the time, and there were over ten thousand people working there. They processed our wool from the raw material, from scouring all the way through to the finished product, one process after another, until it came out the other end of the mill as yarn and cloth.

Barb wasn't invited, so she went shopping. I didn't have a clue what I was in for; I thought I'd duck in and see where our wool went, maybe talk to a couple of people, but not take them away from their work or anything like that. A chap from the Kanebo Mill came down to get me, and this big air-conditioned car arrived at the hotel where we were staying. We pulled up at this big luxury-looking building and there was Sochi in a suit and ten girls waiting for me outside with a big sign above them that read, 'Welcome Mr Tindall to Kanebo Mill'. It was embarrassing, I didn't know what to do. I didn't know if I should go along and shake their hands or say something or what, and they were all bowing and I was bowing in return, and they're bowing back and I was wondering who stopped first. Every bow was returned by another bow!

Eventually they led me into the building and showed me their section, and then I was passed on to another bloke and another building, and it was the same all over again— 'Welcome to Mr Tindall', three times in three different buildings, and there had to be five or six girls outside of the entrance each time, all smiling and bowing. I still didn't know what to do.

At the end of the last building tour, they took me upstairs. A whole lot of these wool experts and buying experts were waiting for me; they grilled me, talking to me about this free trade agreement business that was happening at the time, which I didn't really know much about.

Lach and I had just sold our wool, and on the way over I had received a telegram with the prices. I was explaining to them that it was hard to produce wool in our country for that sort of money, and they told me that as long as we were silly enough to sell it at that price (and these were their exact words)—if we put it on the market at that price and took what was offered—we deserved as little as we got. I was told they could pay twice as much as that, but why should they when we took what was offered? I reckon I found out more there in a couple of hours, about buying and the price of wool, than I had ever known before.

After I returned to the hotel, Sochi rang us and kindly asked us to dinner at his place. We were picked up from our hotel, and were treated like VIPs. Going up into his unit we walked up these really steep narrow steps. The houses all had these beautiful blue glazed roof tiles and four solid corners made up of four-by-four-inch posts, and the walls were thin, almost paper-like. The walls on some of the houses were just fine sheets of pine with the knots still in them. Sochi told us the idea was that if they had an earthquake, the house would fall down and not hurt you.

Nobody had much of a house in Tokyo; Sochi was second in charge of the second-biggest wool mill in Japan and he had ten thousand people working for him, yet we sat on the floor for dinner. He had another house outside of Tokyo that he would go home to on weekends, and he would stay in Tokyo during the week. He had a housekeeper; his wife was at their home outside Tokyo and he apologised for that, so the housekeeper cooked for us all on a gas ring in the middle of the room. She brought in this little cooking plate and there was a gas cylinder outside with a plastic hose, and she started cooking as we were sitting on the floor.

Sochi was really nice. He didn't even own a car—he wasn't allowed to own one. Unless you owned a carport and could take the car off the street at night, you couldn't own a car in Tokyo. He told us that he commuted to his main home, 100 miles from Tokyo, once a week. He'd get on the train and it would go at 100 mile an hour; everyone stood up as there wasn't enough room for seats. There were no stops; all the passengers got off at the same place and then the train would return express to Tokyo.

Ever tried sitting for two hours on the floor? Barb and I had such sore knees; we moved around on our knees or bum the entire time, this way and that way, and we were in agony. Sochi just sat there perfectly still. I suppose he didn't realise; he was just used to it. Then this housekeeper was kneeling there served us a bit of this and a bit of that; as soon as we ate a bit, she gave us some more of something else. What we were eating I don't know, it was all different. I'd like to go through it again now, but how would I?

We didn't realise at the time how special the experience was. When I came back home and told the agent, he kept questioning me about Sochi taking us to his place; he couldn't believe it. After we returned to Australia we found out that the Japanese would normally take you to a big restaurant, get you anything you want, but they rarely invite you into their home—it was the ultimate compliment.

When the agent had originally given me Sochi's contact details, I'd asked if there was anything I should take him as a present, and I was told to bring a bottle of whisky. Whisky was apparently illegal in Japan at the time. To get it off the boat when we arrived, I carried a coat over my arm with the bottle of whisky tied into it. Those customs blokes must have known, but Sochi thought it was wonderful. So it really was the perfect present to give him as a thankyou.

When we came back to Australia, the other agents found out about what happened at the Kanebo mill with the buyers, and then they started grilling me as well. I don't know why—there were Australian blokes going over from the wool industry all the time and they would surely find out things.

Even though I had nothing to do with the implementation of the Australian Wool Reserve Price Scheme in 1974, I did attempt on two occasions to get up at UGA meetings and have my say. The wool price had been tumbling over the last two decades after the wool boom, and there was concern among some growers that overseas buyers were colluding to keep the price low. Bill Gunn—by then Sir William Gunn, now chairman of the Australian Wool Board—convinced the government to go guarantee on a floor price for wool in 1974. A minimum floor price meant the buyers would have to bid above that price, or the wool would be purchased by the Wool Board which was backed by the government and the wool stockpiled to put onto the market at a later date when the market met the price. It worked well, but the floor price kept creeping up.

At the UGA meetings I told them all that I thought the reserve price should be set at about 5 per cent above the cost of production, so that in the worst-case scenario, if the buyers pulled out or the global price dropped substantially at least costs were covered. But they weren't interested; everyone wanted more. The reserve price was set on 30 June each year.

I wasn't against the scheme, especially after talking to Sochi and the Japanese buyers back at Kanebo. Both times I brought it up I failed to get my motion passed in our local Hughenden branch of the UGA. The government allowed the floor price to continue to rise, and wool growers were happy in the knowledge that they would receive a good minimum price for their wool each year.

The scheme failed spectacularly in 1991, when millions of bales were stockpiled and the market price dropped.

Chapter 42

Julie goes shearing; leaving Limbri

JULIE HAD DECIDED from an early age that she wanted to be a shearer; she had even dressed as a shearer for a fancy dress competition at primary school. Both my girls had worked a lot in our shed. I used to do my own crutching with just one other man, and Julie in particular would come down and I'd load her up a handpiece and she'd try shearing. I didn't want her to do it: if you're a strong girl, I'd say yes; but being slight like she was, I was against it. She reckoned anything a man could do, she could do, but some of my big wethers were heavier than she was. And the rams . . . well. I said to her, 'Julie, it's silly. You're going to try and pull out rams bigger than yourself? Not only pull him out, but hold him with a handpiece in one hand?' She then told me she'd crutch. So I'd load up a handpiece and she learnt to crutch. Crutching is quick work compared to shearing, just removing wool from the sheep's breech and top knot instead of the entire fleece. You finish one and you're onto the next; you can average about four hundred a day in good going, and you're pulling out tons and tons of sheep every day from the pen. I personally would much rather shear.

After school she went and helped a neighbour with their children's correspondence work, as a governess I suppose. She met this bloke Ray who was shearing there, and he was a very good shearer and he agreed to teach her. She left her job and followed the shearers, barrowing (learning to shear) with Ray and working in the shearing sheds, eventually becoming a shearer. They went around shearing together and she got very good at it.

Some of the shearers they were working with didn't like the fact that Ray had 'jumped class', that he was going out with a cocky's daughter, not one of their own. And as far as they were concerned, encouraging a woman to shear was not on. As I've mentioned, lady shearers were unheard of in Australia until 1956 and some of the old prejudices still remained. Ray often had to settle disputes with his fists at the pub after cut-out. Lucky for him, he was a good fighter as well as a good shearer. I didn't have an issue with him; he was always polite when he and Julie came around.

Well, country towns being what they are, it became too tough for them in Hughenden, Blackall and Longreach, so they went down to New South and shore around Moree, where it wasn't so militant. She and Ray eventually went their separate ways, but Julie kept shearing.

The TAFE College at Warwick has a shearing school, and they started up a ladies shearing competition. Julie was getting pretty good at shearing by then, so she decided to enter the first ladies shearing competition at the Warwick Show, and she won. She was then asked by the TAFE College to give demonstrations, showing that even a little girl could still shear a big wether. She had great fun— she was better than most of the students because she had already been shearing every day for weeks and weeks as a full-time shearer.

It eventually got too much for her—her back was aching and she was getting like a string bean. So she took a job in a bank. She now works as a livestock clerk at the local abattoir in Warwick. You can ask her what the carcasses weighed, where they came from, what they paid, where they are going, percentages of everything—it's all kept on computers. She said that she doesn't even have a pencil these days—everything is on computer.

Maree was a real bushie and she just loved horses. After school she trained as a nurse, and she married a very nice chap, but a townie. They had two boys, then split up. She married again and has a third boy. She hates the cold, so she lives near Proserpine, up among the cane fields.

In 1976, at the age of fifty, I retired from council after losing the local election by nine votes. It was close and they had a recount, but I still lost by three votes. I think everyone thought I was putting too much energy into the town, rather than the outer areas of the shire, and those were the people who voted me in or out, the people living out of town. I really enjoyed my sixteen years on the Flinders Shire Council, ten of them as works chairman.

Three years later we sold Limbri. Our daughters had grown up and left the nest by then, and Barb asked me one day, 'What are we stopping out here for? There are a lot better places to live than Hughenden.' I used to just love Hughenden—I was on the council and in the tennis and cricket clubs, and we used to go to everything around the district. Initially I didn't want to leave, but sense prevailed. There are better places to live; I've never regretted living there as long as we did, or moving on when we did.

Lach and I split up the Tindall Brothers partnership; Lach and Marg kept Antrim, and Barb and I sold Limbri to a fellow who had won $250,000 in the casket lottery. He had this money available, his winnings, so he just paid the money up front and we bought a caravan and started looking for somewhere else to settle.

At first we bought 310 acres at Rockhampton, near the Gracemere saleyards, close to where most of Barb's people were. The house left a lot to be desired, but it had beautiful loamy soil and was only ten mile out of Rocky. I could run a few cattle on the place and Barb was closer to her family, but the valuer-general kept putting up the unimproved values on the rates as Rockhampton expanded and neighbours subdivided. So we subdivided as well and put it on the market. We sold the land in about six or eight blocks, and it's all built on now.

We were then looking for places around the area, but they were too small or too large and I thought, 'I'm not going to build up another place at my age.' Barb and I decided we'd like to see a bit of Australia, so we hooked up the caravan and travelled around.

While we were travelling, we called in to see a friend from Longreach who was now living on a few acres at Warwick. It was a real hot day for Warwick; he was complaining and I said, 'Jack, do you want to sell?' It sort of pulled him up and he said, 'Well, I'll discuss it with my family.' We were heading off to the Snowy Mountains for a few weeks, so we put a price on it and said, 'We'll see.'

We bought his 68 acres right on the Condamine River flats, a lovely place called Stoneleigh. At first we thought about setting up an embryo transfer business for cattle, which was just coming in, but after doing a bit of home-work we realised that most people wanted to have the procedure done on their own place rather than transporting their good cows to us. Because there were such beautiful river flats on Stoneleigh, I thought I'd grow lucerne instead and run a few cows there.

Chapter 43

Celebrating the past

FOR YEARS I had been collecting shearing equipment, and by 1981 I had quite a big collection of handpieces and shearing memorabilia. We had a Jackie Howe shearing competition organised by locals when we first came down to Warwick, and just for something different I suggested that I bring my collection along. It created such a stir that I was prevailed upon to take it to a few different shows, and soon I just couldn't keep up with demand.

With only a few cows to look after on 68 acres, I started to travel around to shows and different events with my shearing collection. It was a drawcard for the show—there was lots of interest from old shearers, graziers, people who remembered seeing things being used in the past, even people who didn't know what half of the gear was. I was always answering questions and showing people how the old equipment I'd collected was used. I was very proud of my collection. Of course, knowing a fair bit about shearing and that sort of thing, I started to tell people about the early days of shearing. I'd talk about the big shearing sheds and the shearers' strikes, and stations with big numbers of sheep, like Bowen Downs east of Muttaburra, where they were running 400,000 sheep and marked 117,000 lambs in 1896—a phenomenal number.

Soon I was travelling to about twenty shows, field days and ram sales a year, all over the east coast. There was no cost to whoever was organising the show or field day, except they had to put me up overnight and give me some money for petrol. They seemed to think they were getting a good deal, but I always learnt something new—on every trip someone would tell me about something or give me something for my collection. People often came up and said they had something at home that I might like, and I'd get their phone number and chase it up later.

Demonstrating an 1898 husband-and-wife unit—Mitchell Show 1989.

I didn't feel embarrassed going to somebody's place, and if I saw something I wanted, I didn't feel embarrassed asking them if I could add it to my collection. If they didn't donate it, I'd offer to 'buy it or pinch it'. Of course I never actually pinched anything—people would just laugh when I said that. Ninety-nine per cent of the people I asked did donate their old gear, but I did have to buy at auctions a couple of handpieces that were quite rare.

The owner and his wife at Brenda Station, on the New South Wales–Queensland border, were really interested in the collection. They took us down to their rubbish dump and they were both in there pulling things out and asking if this or that was any good. Brenda was such a historical place. There was plenty of interesting finds that visit to Brenda, but the owners wanted to keep them to recognise the historical significance of their property. I told them what the different things were and how they were used and they explained to me the history of their station, I obtained a lot of information from that visit and an unusual bottle that had once held strychnine pills that had been in a cupboard in the office from about 1920.

I just loved rubbish dumps, especially around a shearing shed, and I've spent a lot of time searching through them for old shearing gear. It sounds odd, to turn up and ask to look at someone's rubbish dump, and people would often look at me a bit funny, until they got to know who I was and what I was after.

I was losing money with all the travelling but I didn't

mind as I talked to people and went to places I wouldn't otherwise have gone to. It used to take me two hours to pack up the full shearing collection on my trailer, then I'd need time to set up at the show, and then repack before heading home. I put tags on everything with some information so people could read a bit about it themselves if I was busy. Occasionally I'd find that something had been lifted; I had some really great old things and someone would take a liking to something and it would just disappear. That was always disappointing, especially if it was letters or old photos—all they had to do was ask for a copy.

With some of my handpiece collection at a field day.

I took my collection to places like church fetes and schools, to raise money. I raised money that way for the School of the Air, the Red Cross and the Royal Flying Doctor Service.

The abattoir near Stoneleigh where Julie works is known by the locals as the Bacon Factory. The abattoir wanted our land, our river flats, to run some cattle and grow crops, but we didn't want to move. So they put a proposition to us: they'd buy it and we'd still be able to live there. We could have the house and tennis courts and workshop, as long as they could grow their crops on the river flats. They didn't want the house, so we sold our cattle and just lived there after they bought it and it didn't cost us a thing for ten years.

Just imagine if you could sell your house, invest the money and still live there for nothing, and the new owners would paint it and maintain it. This suited both the new owners and us. They had two hundred cattle running there; if one of the cows was calving and got into trouble, I'd pull the calf or at least ring them up and let them know what was going on.

We had financial security, a maintained home, and time to spend with family.

Chapter 44

Moving on

AFTER YEARS OF almost constant back pain, that I blamed on riding rough horses rather than shearing, I woke up one morning with the pain having spread down one leg, and the leg was going numb. I went to the doctor and was diagnosed with a compressed disk in the lower back and had to be operated on. They removed part of my hip, fashioned it into a disc and put it in place in my spine with four screws and two U-bolts.

I was right after that, but it meant I could no longer mow the vast lawns at Stoneleigh, as the jarring motion brought the pain back. We'd had thirty-one happy years at Stoneleigh, but Barb also felt that the house was getting too big for her to keep, so in 2011 we decided to move into a new house at a nearby retirement village, Regency Park. We've been happy here; I'm always tinkering, making things and helping the maintenance men around the place—I just love it.

Before we moved, I sold most of my shearing collection to one of the places I showed my collection, the Jondaryan Woolshed (Appendix 2). We had an auction to get rid of all the stuff we had—tractors and scoops, other things I'd collected, furniture, everything. I had to cry, but I had no option; we couldn't store it all in our new home. We got an agent to sell it all at the local showground. People came from everywhere. I kept a few bits and pieces, things that were important to me. I still sometimes go looking for something I used to have and then remember it's gone. That is a strange sad feeling.

Just across the street from where we live now is the Warwick TAFE College. There is a chap there, David Wyllie, who used to be the shearing instructor at the TAFE; when I was travelling around with my collection he would often take his learner shearers to see my collection at the different shows; he even brought some of his students out to our home at Stoneleigh. About fifteen years ago, he was involved in a car accident and had to have his right arm cut off between the elbow and the shoulder, and of course he couldn't shear then.

He rang me one morning in 2008, a few years after the accident, and said he wanted to go back shearing; thinking he was joking, I said, 'Yeah, and you're going to be playing the violin at the same time.' He said, 'No, I'm fair dinkum.' We had a few old sheep at Stoneleigh and I said, 'Well, come out and we'll see what we can do.' We put the sheep in the yard and went through the motions of shearing a sheep—holding it, rolling it over, taking off the belly wool and so on. I said, 'Before I can do anything, you need to go to Brisbane and get a sort of sock made up to fit over your stump. I also asked him to find a half-inch steel screw that I could wind a threaded lock nut onto. When he came back I started making hooks and things.

The first problem we tackled was holding the sheep. I made a prosthetic arm with a C-section metal hook on the end. The C-section can go over the sheep's leg, so David could hold the sheep in place as he shore. Our next problem was that the arm wouldn't stop spinning around when you put pressure on it. I made some big straps and put those on it, and it seemed to work. Next, I sent him down to the saddler to get this brace made up—great big thick straps that went around his middle and over his shoulder. Now when we put the prosthetic arm and hook on, it worked.

David took it down to Brisbane to show the amputee specialists and they said, 'Who the hell made this for you?' and he said, 'Oh, some old shearer bloke out in the west.' I didn't patent it—I supposed there wasn't much call for one-armed shearers.

David is back shearing. He doesn't do as many sheep as he used to, but he was invited over to Norway about six years ago to demonstrate how he shore with it; two years ago he was invited to England to demonstrate how he shears and to show people that just because you only have one arm doesn't mean you can't do things.

Now there is a man with a ton of guts; he never gave up. Here's a man with his arm knocked off and he is still shearing a sheep.

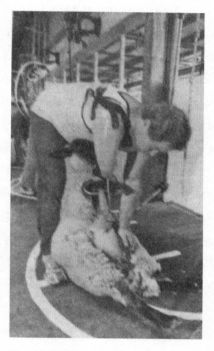

David Wyllie shearing.

We've just become great-grandparents for the third time, and we appreciate every day we spend with our family. I'm still close to all the brothers and my sister Ethel. Arthur passed away a couple of years ago, but all the rest of us are still here and just love getting together and having a few laughs.

The first block Dad owned, Red Knob, was sold in the 1950s and was renamed Ve Jovis by the new owners; it's a bit of a landmark property out on the old dingo fence. Godfrey sold Beatrice in the 1950s and bought another property up at Muttaburra called Hillview, which has since been sold. Arthur was on Thurles Park and bought the block next door, Bald Hills; those places have since been sold too. Brian, the baby of the family, bought the place next door to Gaza, Janet Downs, and his sons Richard and Doug now run both places with their families. Ethel and David's son John still runs Verastone.

Not long after we left Limbri, Lach sold Antrim and moved back west with his family. He bought Darr River Downs at Longreach, which his son Cam and three grandsons now run with their families. Lach's eldest boy Robert and his family are now on what was Dad's last property, MacFarlane Downs. Both Lach and Godfrey and their wives are retired in Toowoomba, near Ethel and Colin, not far from us; we get to see them fairly often.

Dad took a risk going out to Red Knob in the 1920s, but he showed us how to work hard. Three generations of his descendants are still working and living out there. Dad bought MacFarlane in 1940 and the family have had it for over seventy years.

Our family had always run sheep; we were almost exclusively sheep men, until the dingoes came in. We didn't have any dingo trouble when Dad first bought MacFarlane, but now it is so bad that the family have had to shift out of sheep; now Robert can only run cattle. They have dingoes as far east as Tambo now, and in the last ten or so years people have had to move out of sheep.

So what is the future . . . the future of sheep and wool in Australia? As I've said, sheep have all but gone from that western country—the wild dogs have them beat—but there is still plenty of sheep and wool producers around in the southern states.

As for wool, when synthetics first came in after the Korean War, everyone threw their hands up in the air and said wool wouldn't be in demand anymore, but the doomsayers were proven wrong. The problem today is that wool's sold on the open market; we don't say what price we want—the buyers just come along and offer us money. You can withdraw it from sale if you're game, but most don't. They just have to face the market, that's all there is to it.

But what's the option if you pull it off the market? These blokes, the buyers go, 'Bugger ya—we'll buy another line.' Because someone else, another grower, is always willing to take the cheaper money. I think it's the same as growing fruit and vegetables, or most agricultural produce that goes to market—it's free trade and you just hope you can put better quality into the market than your mate can.

Protectionism was a failure. The reserve price scheme was scrapped in the early 1990s, and I still maintain the base price they put on wool should have been just above our costs of production. With protectionism, prices went up and they kept raising the base price, following the higher prices, and didn't allow for falls in the market. I was really crooked about that. Then prices started coming down. Five million bales were stacked up, and when the buyers found out there was so much wool stockpiled, the price fell further. People were going to the wall. If they'd maintained the base price just above cost of production it might have been different, but there are wiser blokes than me in the job. I remember saying at one of the UGA meetings, 'If they stop buying our wool, what do you do?'

I knew some people who didn't sell wool for two years after the scheme crashed because they weren't prepared to accept the lower prices, but then they had to start selling again because the banks told them to. Interest rates were at record highs at the time, and those interest rates were killing them.

I think wool has got a future. There are great people in the industry. I've seen a few things, gone through a few of life's ups and downs, and ultimately I like to see the good in every person. To me, whether you're a shearer or you're a grazier, there is good in every person. There is probably only a small percentage of people who aren't genuine, and you work out who those ones are. I'm thankful the class warfare has abated since 1956; it shouldn't be us and them. It's just us—all of us.

We've got a future right enough.

THE TINDALL COLLECTION

Appendix 1: Rare finds—becoming a collector
Appendix 2: Jondaryan Woolshed
Appendix 3: Class war—shearers versus graziers
Appendix 4: Combs, cutters and the wide comb debate
Appendix 5: Growing fine wool
Appendix 6: Mulesing

Appendix 1

Rare finds—becoming a collector

THE 1956 SHEARERS' strike was when I started my collection of shearing equipment. I was shearing out at the Dunluce shed, west of Hughenden on the Mount Isa line, and I was just poking around the rubbish heap one afternoon for something to do and came across an 1888 handpiece, an old brass one, and I thought, 'I wonder how that works.' I'd always enjoyed figuring out how things work. On weekends or at night I'd work on it, and I finally got it going.

From then on, whenever I went to another shed I'd go down to the rubbish pits around the shed, and I was finding all sorts of curious things—anything from old shears to wool hooks and tally books. This started off my collection of shearing equipment and memorabilia that continued for another fifty years.

I was lucky enough to find some important things in my time. The Leslie Brothers came into the Darling Downs in about 1864, and they took up land just outside of Warwick. It was quite a big place that went out around and included the town of Killarney. I went to look at the rubbish heap one day at the Canning Downs shed, the first place the Leslies settled, and I picked up an old original Canning Downs bale stencil that was badly damaged and had parts of it missing. It was all scrunched up, but I made what was missing and soldered it all together.

Another thing I found was a sheep nose brand—they used to brand sheep on the nose with a hot iron. I didn't even know what it was to start with, until someone gave me an old photo taken in 1907, showing blokes nose branding. They had a rail about two foot off the ground, with two pegs in it six inches apart all along the rail. They'd catch a ram and push it's neck between the pegs and a bloke would come along the front with a hot iron and brand them all on the nose while the brand was hot. Eventually I got the registered brand book, which had all of the registered brands put out by the Queensland Department of Primary Industries. I ended up with five of those brands; as far as I know, nobody had ever found one before—or possibly, just like me, they didn't know what they were.

ROCKWOOD HUGHENDEN 1907
HOT IRON NOSE BRANDING

Hot-iron nose branding—Hugh Tindall Collection.

I collected five different sorts of hand-operated shearing plants, what they called the husband-and-wife units. One sort had a big bike wheel; another had gear cogs on it. I got them working again, and after I retired I used to give demonstrations of shearing with an old 1890 handpiece. By then I had nearly seventy different sorts of overhead gear and handpieces.

Back then ordinary people invented and improved shearing gear; they were all just trying different things to see what would work best. There were rotary handpieces, handpieces running off compressed air—many different methods were invented and tried out. A lot of the early handpieces weren't much good; the better ones survived and were used.

If I said 'Silver', 'Smoko' or 'Simplex', people today wouldn't know what I was talking about, but they were brands of overhead gear and handpieces. The Smoko was very rare; it was cast iron and I had learnt to shear on one. I did eventually get a Smoko, but I had to pay eight hundred dollars for it at an auction back in November 1994 in Narromine—I really wanted it. Barb could have got a diamond ring for that, but my argument was that my Smoko handpiece generated more interest than a diamond ring would have.

Another rare handpiece, the Grace, was made in Sweden—like most of the handpieces at the time, it was invented in Australia but manufactured overseas. One type of Grace handpiece had a clockwork system: you'd wind it up with a piece of string and then pull it out and take a blow; you'd shear one part of the sheep, but then you had to wind it up again. The Silver handpiece was also very rare, named after the fellow who invented it. It had three pistons working in a circle like a rotary engine and was air driven.

Frederick York Wolseley, an Irish inventor working on a sheep station in the Riverina, was responsible for the development of many shearing units and shearing pieces. He experimented first with a modification based on horse clippers, and then advanced to an individual wool-clipping machine. He was the first to invent a satisfactory handpiece. A few people had tried it and spent years on it, but he just persisted until he got the first one working properly and reliably. When the Wolseley handpiece first came out in 1888 it was made of brass, like the one I found at Dunluce, but it was too hot to hold, so the shearers used to cut a piece of felt and wrap it around the handpiece—they often cut up their hat for this purpose. The brass ones only lasted two years, and in 1890 Wolseley put the same handpieces out in chrome steel. He was successful enough to buy later refinements from fellow graziers and shearers as modifications happened, so his company would gain the financial benefit and the credit for them.

The English had hand shears that were brought out with the First Fleet, and it was very rare for any to be made in Australia. Wolseley manufactured his handpieces overseas, mainly in Sheffield, England, an area renowned in the late nineteenth century for producing the best knives, blades and cutlery in the Commonwealth. Precision steel manufacturing was of a higher quality in England, and also in Norway and Sweden, than in Australia at the time.

A bloke called John Howard, funnily enough, was an innovative engineer that Wolseley employed for years, and in 1888 he created the one-degree fall in the comb and cutter grinder from the centre of the disc to the outside, which creates a hollow when grinding comb and cutters.

Shearers used to grind a hollow into their hand shears so they cut better, but with the advent of handpieces, the fall in the grinding wheel made it possible with combs and cutters to also have a hollow between them. A small hollow is found between the two ends in clippers, and even good-quality scissors, that results in a better cut when the two blades join. There is not as much friction between the two as would otherwise result.

A lot of people think combs and cutters are dead flat;

but they aren't—Howard designed a grinding wheel or disc with a fall of 1 per cent from the centre that enables shearers to grind out an area in the middle. If you've got a flat disc, and you've got a comb and cutter that you're grinding on it, it will rub the whole surface evenly. If you are using a grinder with a fall from the centre to the outside, you can get a tiny hollow grind, which is exaggerated when you join the comb and cutter together on the handpiece.

Jackie Howe is the man in the centre of the back row; the tall man on the right is Alexander Jack Lavercombe, whose descendant gave me a copy of this photo. The men are wearing leather pants, gloves and aprons because it was prickly pear country (Photograph thought to have been taken near Mitchell around 1894.).

Over a period of time travelling around and displaying my collection I had old fellas come up and tell me shearing stories—for example, how Jackie Howe used to carry around a wooden box full of oiled wool to put his handpiece in when it got too hot. Blow me down if I didn't actually find a couple of those boxes out at Walgett in New South Wales. I'd heard about them but hadn't seen one before then.

Jackie Howe is renowned in Australia's shearing history for shearing 321 sheep with hand blades at Alice Downs on 10 October 1892, an incredible feat. But what irks me about this piece of our history is how it's been exaggerated. Those sheep, according to the tally book, were lambs, but it has become part of the folklore surrounding that day that he shore full-wool ewes. In fact it was the end of shearing, when traditionally the lambs were shorn and it is listed in the tally book under the 'Lambs' column.

Tally book from Alice Downs Station showing Jackie Howe shore 321 lambs in one day.

Lambing would commence on 1 April and they were shorn at the start of October, so they would have had only six months of wool on them. The ewes at Alice Downs only cut three pounds, seven ounces (just over one and a half kilograms) each that year, whereas a ewe today with improved genetics would cut four or five kilos of wool; the lambs he shore wouldn't have had about nine ounces of wool on them, making it quick shearing. Not to take anything away from the man—it was incredible for a shearer to shear with blades 321 lambs in a day—but they were lambs, not fully grown ewes.

There were all sorts of stories told about Howe, like when he ran a 100-yard (90-metre) foot race and he stopped to have a yarn with someone and still won the race! But I guess people love a legend, and like all good shearing yarns, they get bigger and better with time.

Another odd thing I found were ram emasculators. If at the end of the season studs had rams left unsold, they would put these giant emasculators—two thick pieces of steel, about five to six inches long with a screw bolt on either side—on their purse and turn them into wethers. When the emasculators dropped off, you'd find them in the grass with the scrotum bag attached. I had about fifty of the contraptions from out at Welltown Stud, the other side of Goondiwindi, and over the years I gave one to every museum who asked for one.

I also heard that up till 1880, people used to wash sheep in a big long race for two or three days before shearing them. Back then the wool was only an inch and a half (four centimetres) long at shearing, so it would have been quite easy to wash; since then, genetic breeding has increased the amount of wool on sheep. Every ten feet along the race they'd have great big showerheads to pump water over the sheep and remove the dust. The shearers used to have to get in there and wash the sheep. I found one out near Aramac, 1000 miles from the coast, and it's all still there but no longer used. The people who were out there knew what it was used for.

Why do people collect? Some see the possibility of future profit. Some collect because they like the items; some because the items are pretty; some because they are rare. The thing about collecting is you can lose all sense of responsibility. You're never really satisfied, and if you're not careful, you can throw discretion out the window. I started collecting initially because I wanted to know how the shearing equipment worked, and then I wanted to know its history. I started to research, asking people who might know. Sometimes I was told things that weren't true, but gradually I found out the facts. Sometimes I jumped to the wrong conclusions, but I enjoyed learning the truth eventually.

In twenty-five years of showing my collection I travelled over 310,000 miles and virtually wore out three utilities. For the first ten years I charged nothing for demonstrations; then, after it was offered, I started to charge fuel and accommodation costs. Very few items I had to buy; the main cost was travelling to get items I had been told about. One of the saddest parts of collecting was being told about something and then, after many miles of travelling, getting there only to find out that shortly before my arrival someone had come in with a bulldozer and buried our history.

As well as shearing equipment, I collected bells. I had over three hundred bells from all round the world. I just like them, probably from the days when we used to go out early in the morning to catch the horses in the dark from the sound of their bells. I like small bells and big bells—they all have a different sound. I started collecting bells from different countries—I had bells from Russia and China, mostly horse or stock bells; I had Austrian and Russian sleigh bells. Some of them were very rare.

Then I used to make a few. The old pumps in the bores were solid brass, and if I got a bit of brass tubing out of a compensator at the top of the pump, I could make three bells out of it. The brass alone was worth a lot of money.

I gave Barb's sister Sue a little bell and she put it over her front door; every time the door opened, it would ring. She woke up one night when she heard the bell and thought, 'Somebody is inside.' She woke Kevin, her husband, and when he got up to investigate, the thieves scarpered. They had come in a window and opened the front door in case they needed to escape in a hurry and that's what woke her up. Kevin raced out and the robbers took off. She is very fond of that little bell now.

Appendix 2

Jondaryan Woolshed

JONDARYAN WOOLSHED, OUTSIDE of Toowoomba, was formerly run by volunteers as a display of days gone by, and is still used today as a permanent museum.

At one time Jondaryan Station had over two hundred thousand sheep and not a fence on the place—they would have needed over a hundred shepherds back then. All sheep were shepherded in the early days, by shepherds and their dogs. They had their own 'shepherd's box', which was their home while they were out with their flock. It was a tall bed-shaped box, with two wheels at the front for portability, and two legs at the back—it looked a bit like a long wheelbarrow. A tarpaulin formed the roof and sides; it could be rolled up on each side, for access and to allow a breeze through. The tarp or camp sheet was quite weatherproof and rainproof; it could get cold out there at night, but the tarp kept the box warm when it was rolled down. The men would cut a bullock hide into strips and plait or weave it together to form a mattress, and then put two or three sheepskins on that to sleep on.

At dusk the sheep would be put into a break, which was a yard made out of trees lying on top of one another, constructed over the years and added to and improved by shepherds over time. The shepherd used to peg his dogs across the open side and sleep in his shepherd's box in the middle of the sheep. The reason for this was that if dingoes or Aborigines came along and wanted some mutton, the sheep would stir and the shepherd would know what was going on.

The shepherd would walk out with his sheep in the morning, generally water them at midday and then walk them back in the evening to the break, or he'd spend the day moving them on to the next camp. He had to shift camp regularly, because if they stayed in the same place for too long dermatitis or pneumonia could go through the camp. So he'd shift camp every seven to ten days—he just put his cooking utensils and supplies in the box and wheeled it along from place to place. A shepherd never had horses, he only had his dogs. Each week or ten days the owner would bring out fresh provisions and check how the sheep were doing. It must have been a lonely life for the shepherd.

Loading wool at Jondaryan Woolshed in 1894—Hugh Tindall Collection.

Over time, the original station was subdivided into smaller and smaller farms, but people still used to bring their sheep to the woolshed to shear. In its heyday, in the late 1800s, there was a village of three hundred people living at the station— builders, carpenters, blacksmiths, horse breakers, even a butcher's shop, where they used to kill a bullock every day to feed everybody. Their set-up included a steam engine that pumped water out of the river up to the butcher's shop; in summer they had a cooler, which had water dripping down the sides like a big Coolgardie safe. Then they had a wind-mill with a 60-foot-long chain with a mob of little buckets on it to scoop the water up out of the river and tip it out into a tank twenty feet off the ground. All this gear was still there when they sold off the original homestead block twenty years ago, and I went out to the auction to have a look at it.

In 1972 the locals ran a 'shearers' feast' to raise money for the Jondaryan State School, and to celebrate over one hundred years since the first shearing at the shed. The feast was so successful that they held a public meeting to form an association to create a living pioneer station museum at the woolshed. The following year the owner offered the association the woolshed and twelve acres of land for the people of Jondaryan to restore and preserve the buildings and heritage.

Nobody out at Jondaryan then had much idea of sheep and shearing equipment. In 1982 I started to take some of my collection over for the Australian Heritage Festival, which always started on the last weekend in August and went for ten days. They gave me some space in the old woolshed to set up my shearing gear; to start with, I only took the lighter stuff and the hand-operated gear.

The Jondaryan woolshed is the same sort of shed as the famous one out at Tuppal Station at Tocumwal in the Riverina region of New South Wales—the same size and same T-shape. It was originally about 300 foot long and 90 foot wide. It had two boards with fifty-two stands in total; there was a dump press, a wool room and woolpress in the T part, and great big doors at the end to unload the fleeces. All the wool bins and classing tables were in the middle, together with shed pens for holding sheep to be shorn. There were also sheep pens all along the back and in the middle, and counting-out pens outside each stand. When the shearer finished shearing a sheep he would pop them down a slide and they'd land in the counting-out pen ready to be recorded against the shearer's tally.

When they were building the shed, there were two men cutting three hundred thousand shingles to go on the roof, but in 1880 the owners ordered galvanised iron from England and sold the shingles. For the first shearing they put tarps on for a roof; then they put on the iron when it arrived. All of the corrugated iron was pre-drilled in England—every sheet on every second corrugate had a bolt in it, so the roof could never blow off. Just after the Second World War the owners took one end off the shed and sold the iron because there was a shortage of it and it was quite valuable, but in about 1978 they replaced it and screwed it all back on.

There were three wool tables, and originally two Wilding screw presses, replaced by a single, more efficient Ferrier press in 1890. There was also a big steam engine sitting alongside the shed that initially ran the mechanised shearing gear.

The woolshed was the perfect place to talk about how shearing used to be done and how it had changed over the years. I used to go there and talk about shearing equipment; show the visitors how to set dingo traps; and go into the sheep yards and demonstrate how to draft, count sheep at speed, things like that.

Not long after I first went out there, I put in a line shaft with permanent individual 1920 Wolseley overhead gear and we started running shearing competitions; I'd give a running commentary on the shearing in what has now become a permanent auditorium. We later put in four electric stands for competitions. We brought in exhibition shearers; they usually didn't start until nine o'clock in the morning and they got paid for the day and loved it. The shearers came back every year.

Showing visitors how to set a dingo trap.

I talked about shearing and outback history. I had a bike-operated husband-and-wife shearing unit and I would ask a volunteer to get on and pedal; I showed them how the other hand-operated displays worked. After a few years, they put in two posts and jacked up a wagon wheel with a belt for power, and I'd shear with that. They got me on stage to talk while someone was shearing, and I'd talk about droughts and the history of the sheds. I could talk all day; when the shearers knocked off, I'd talk about the history of the place if people were interested.

When Barb and I went out to Jondaryan, we used to camp in the shearers' quarters, or in our own caravans if there wasn't room in the quarters. The old shearers' quarters were really something when they first put them up in 1879. They were twelve foot square with a big verandah out the front.

Most of the people who attended the festival brought their own caravans, and they had a couple of cooks out there who'd put on really good meals for us all. We had great big campfires, and a lot of people would sit up talking till the early hours of the morning. Someone would be telling yarns, playing a saw or violin or squeezebox. Barb came for two years—it was good fun, and we both enjoyed going to the festival.

In 2005 the Jondaryan Woolshed committee bought my collection to display at Jondaryan. I was initially happy about that as it was getting too much with all the travelling and Barb was at home alone a lot of the time. Sometimes she'd come with me but not every time. She didn't like staying at home by herself; it was pretty isolated at Stoneleigh with nobody around. So I decided to sell my collection to Jondaryan.

I haven't gone out to Jondaryan in a while, because I was a bit upset about what they did with my collection after I sold it to them. They got it for virtually nothing. I could have split it up and shared it between museums, because Shear Outback at Hay wanted some of it and the Stockman's Hall of Fame at Longreach wanted some of it, but I wanted to keep it all together.

My understanding was that they were going to build a dedicated shed at Jondaryan to put the whole collection in, sealed up to protect it but with everything still on display for people to look through. I went out about ten years ago and half the collection was lying on the floor; rain can come in the southern side during storms, and the mesh still lets the birds and the dust in.

Then they got in an authority on museums from Brisbane, and they split up parts of the collection. There's a bit here and a bit there; it's all over the place, in seven different sheds. They set up a bike trail and you're supposed to go from one to the other.

I said to them, 'Look, if I go to a museum, I want to see all the same gear together, so I can study the differences between them.' Say, in a car museum—you'd want to see all the Holdens together. I don't want to see one here and one over there; I want to see them together, so I can compare them. I turned my back on it in the last few years—I don't go back much anymore.

Appendix 3

Class war—shearers versus graziers

I'VE ALWAYS LOVED finding out about shearing history, and I managed to find out many things over time, from talking to other shearers, hearing stories about how things used to be done.

Back in the late nineteenth and early twentieth centuries, a lot of shearers and shed hands would ride out on pushbikes a week before a big shed was due to start shearing. In the really big sheds out west, they'd want, say, eighty-eight shearers, and two hundred shearers might turn up wanting a job. Roustabouts, pressers, cooks and other shed staff were also hired, not just shearers, but often there still wasn't enough jobs for the number of men who turned up. If they weren't initially employed, the men were allowed to stop there and were tuckered for three days, but then they had to get off the place. However, they knew that some of the shearers who'd been hired weren't near as good as they thought they were and they'd get the sack, so some of these blokes would stop there a bit longer in the hope to pick up these jobs.

When you had mobs of men together and you didn't know a lot about them, word of mouth carried a lot of weight. The managers would find out who the good shearers were and who wasn't. Or if a man had a reputation for causing trouble, he wouldn't be picked. Those who weren't chosen had to tramp or pushbike to the next station that had shearing coming up—there was no other means of transport.

The first time I saw a shearer with a car was in 1942. By then most still came out with the mail truck or the contractor. Back in the 1800s they either came out in a mail wagon or Cobb & Co coach, or walked. Then in the 1890s the pushbike became available, so that was how a lot of them got around. If they had the breeze behind them, they'd put up four sticks and create a sail using their swag cover, and let the wind carry them along—they called such sails 'dreadnoughts'. They weren't travelling on very good roads, but they only travelled along slowly, and you were right as long as there weren't any bullock wagon tracks in the mud, or lots of loose bulldust or anything to upset the bike. All this, of course, went out when cars and trucks came in and it was easier to get around.

The conflict between graziers and shearers is a long story, but essentially shearers always wanted higher wages and graziers rarely wanted to pay them higher wages. There were shearers' strikes all through the 1890s. It was tough to make a living for both shearers and graziers. Let's face it— in 1891 a lot of things were tough. The Australian Workers Union (AWU) was formed in the wake of the 1894 shearers' strike.

The mechanisation of sheds was the main reason for the 1891 strike. Sheep numbers had increased in Australia in the late 1800s as more land opened up and the demand for Australian wool grew, and there was a real need to invent a faster way to get the wool off.

Sir Samuel McCaughey, the man who brought the Vermont sheep to Australia, was the first to mechanise his shed in 1888; he wanted the new Wolseley shearing machines on his property, Dunlop Station, down on the Darling River out past Bourke. Dunlop had the world's first overhead shearing plant, but there wasn't any overhead shafting, steel-lined shafts putting power to the handpieces, they used a giant loop of rope off a steam engine. There was no way to shear other than with hand shears till after 1888; there was no shafting, of the kind we have in sheds now, on the original Dunlop machines—they simply had a loop of rope running up and down the shed at twenty mile an hour, coming off a steam engine. They shore 184,000 sheep that year with forty motorised stands. McCaughey also owned the place next door, Toorale, together with another place down the river, Coree; he owned about two and a half million acres along the Darling.

Wolseley developed and installed the first rope-driven overhead shearing unit, but it caused endless problems, with many rope breakages, not all of them accidental. The shearers kept cutting the rope that ran the overhead gear, because the new system was considered a threat to the livelihood of the shearers as less of them were needed. When it was installed at Dunlop, an ex-sailor was engaged to splice together the ropes when they broke. The rope-driven overhead shearing unit only lasted a year or two, but it was the forerunner for the development of other mechanical shearing units. The overhead gear was then changed to steel line shafts. There were only a few sheds in Australia that ever put in the rope like they did at Dunlop, but I've never found out where the other sheds were.

Instead of shearing forty to eighty sheep a day with blades, depending on how good they were, the shearers were now shearing a hundred. Not as many shearers were needed for as long, so what were they going to do—sit around at the pub? They went on strike, because they reckoned the new technology would eventually put too many shearers out of work. Eventually, though, the shearers recognised the advantages of mechanical shearing, and the overhead shearing units revolutionised the industry.

The 1894 strike was the most violent. When the price of wool dropped 20 per cent almost overnight to only a penny a pound, because of depressed prices in England, the graziers said they couldn't afford to pay the shearers' the same wages. Whether they could actually afford it or not I wouldn't know, but they pulled the wages down. The shearers weren't going to be in that and there was a big strike. The shearers went around and 'let the red steer go', burning the pastoralists out. A bunch of shearers would be walking along the road beside a big body of grass and one of them would drop a match, and suddenly a fire would break out behind them. Which one of them did it? Nobody knew. Or they'd go out to a big shed at night and burn it down; one of the sheds was apparently full of sheep ready for the next day's shearing. Several large sheds were torched and some of the graziers put armed guards on them day and night. It was very vicious and militant.

If you were a grazier or pastoralist at that time, you just didn't talk to the shearers. The shearers didn't want to be seen talking to the graziers either, so it wasn't a one-way ticket. Both sides would do what they felt they had to do to survive. It was very much an 'us and them' mentality, on both sides. It was a class war.

On those big places, there was rarely an owner present, just a manager to give instructions, and they were tough. I knew one manager in Blackall when I was shearing in the 1950s; if he was going into town, 50 mile away in the car, and he agreed to give a station hand or shearer a lift, he'd drop them on the edge of town—he wouldn't drive up the street and be seen with him. It was just ridiculous. He didn't want to be seen to be consorting with the enemy. For some of the cockies, graziers and managers out west—especially if they or their families had been subject to shearer militancy in the past—that was how they saw the shearers, as the enemy. I think it almost goes back to convict days. The original settlers were from England, and many of them brought the class-consciousness out with them; they looked down on the shearers as almost second-class citizens.

Appendix 4

Combs, cutters and the wide comb debate

THE INTRODUCTION OF wide combs into Australia caused the 1983 shearers' strike. A wide comb is more than two and a half inches (63.5 mm) in width. Shearers were using wide combs a hundred years ago in New Zealand, and they were 10 to 20 per cent faster than the narrow combs, but they weren't allowed to use them in Australia. If New Zealand shearers brought wide combs into the sheds, they'd find the expert would 'accidentally' break them and they had to use narrow combs like everyone else.

The AWU has been a big part of shearing in Australia. New Zealand shearers didn't have the same type of formal union representation, and when they came over the Ditch they were often reluctant to become members of the AWU, which was also the cause of many a dispute over the years between Aussie and Kiwi shearers.

The Kiwis were brought up using the wide comb. It's easier to shear with, because it's faster, but it takes a bit of getting used to. It takes a whole different way of moving around the sheep—with the narrow comb, you used to 'scrunch' the sheep up to draw the wool together so you could get more onto the comb. As the sheep unfurled, the strips where the narrower comb had been would also unfurl and be wider than the width of the narrow comb.

The graziers were happy with the shearers using the wide combs, because they were going to get their sheep shorn that much quicker. It wasn't going to change the cost of actually shearing the sheep, because the shearers were paid per numbers shorn, but it would cut down the number of days' work for the roustabouts and other workers who were in the shed, by 10 per cent at least. Some shearers started using wide combs in sheds. The shed workers weren't so happy if they didn't have another shed to go to straight away.

An AWU organiser down in New South started the 1983 strike over wide combs, and the shearers followed him like a lot of sheep—until they found out, by trying the wide combs, that they were better than the narrow combs. The arguments put forward by the unions as a reason for the strike were very weak, I thought. They reckoned it was harder to shear with the wide combs, but nothing that stood up under scrutiny. I reckon the reason the wide combs weren't used earlier in Australia was international jealousy. There was no real reason for the shearers to be opposed to it. It was like driving a three-ton truck instead of a five-ton truck and being paid by the yardage—it's no harder to drive and you're getting paid by the number of sheep you shore or the number of yards you cart.

I wouldn't know another shearer other than me who would now use the old narrow gear, and I only use it to demonstrate how it worked. Once the shearers were used to the wide comb, it was easier and quicker to shear with. Everyone now uses them to shear in Australia, and if you're not shearing two hundred sheep a day with wide combs you're dragging the chain.

Appendix 5

Growing fine wool

WE ALWAYS RAN merinos—there was nothing out in our country but merinos until the last thirty years. Merinos are tough, they can cope with harsh conditions, and they have a fine type of wool which is still highly sought after by the wool mills. We had hoggets and wethers, which were kept for both their wool and their meat, but now with less paid for wool they are not kept as much. A hogget is a lamb with two permanent teeth that have come up, and their meat tends to have a more mature taste than a lamb once they have permanent teeth. But you'd never talk about buying a wether or a hogget for their wool now.

Wool gets finer, and there is less of it, as the wether gets older. Wool also becomes finer if the sheep is stressed, like in a drought. 'Fine' refers to the thickness of the strand of wool and is used to class the fleece as more is generally paid for finer wool. Since the 1960s it has been measured in microns—one micron is one-millionth of a metre. Prior to that, wool was roughly classified by eye (by the buyer and the classer) as strong, medium or fine. You didn't put a strong wool in with a fine one; you kept them apart as they were chalk and cheese.

The wool used to be given a number according to its [fineness]. If you washed and cleaned a pound of wool and you could spin it for 680 yards, then it would be classed as 68. If it spun out 700 yards, it was classed as 70. We used to say 64–68 was medium to fine, 60 was strong, and 58 was really strong. Wool classified as 72 was much finer, like a cobweb. Nowadays, with the new measurement system, 24–28 micron is more or less the really strong wool, while 18–20 is medium fine, and then down to about 11 is ultra-fine, but they might only get a few pound of wool off the sheep at that micron, when they skirt the pieces out of the fleece.

Out in the west in my time, fine fleece would have been about 18 to 20 micron. Out there, to make it economical, you needed to get at least ten pound (four and a half kilos) of wool from an ordinary wether and eight pound (three and a half kilos) from a ewe, so you went for sheep with stronger types of wool. If you went too fine you might get good money for it, but you wouldn't have enough to fill the bale.

Both drought and wet weather can change wool. Too much moisture in warm weather can turn the wool green, but when you've been in a drought, the wool is all matted down on the skin until such time as the drought breaks; then the wool grows up healthy underneath, like a plant. In poor years, or if the sheep is stressed, the wool will become finer and less will be grown; but you wouldn't do that on purpose—it would tend to be 'tender' or weak in the staple (length of fleece from the skin) which reduced the value of the fleece.

In good years you get longer staple and stronger wool, with more weight. Sometimes in hard times you'll get noticeable lines across the staple sample, the sample of wool the classer pulls off the fleece to class it, which indicates tender wool. You'll see classers flicking the staple—pulling it out and flicking it with their finger, to test whether it will break or not.

If the sheep has been really sick during the year, part of the sheep's fleece will sometimes just break and fall off. The outer part will be poorly grown, with a break in it, but the wool closer to the skin will be better grown, almost two types of fleece from the same sheep, and the wool will be downgraded in price accordingly.

Appendix 6

Mulesing

I HAD A woman ring me from England in 1982. I don't know what it cost her, but she had been told I had been a sheep farmer and that I knew a bit about mulesing. She said, 'We are going to stop this horrific barbaric practice you sheep farmers are doing over there.'

I let her go on for a while and then I said, 'One of these days you come out to Australia. You'll have to pay your own fare, but I can show you what actually happens.'

She ignored this and told me we should get the sheep in every day to check them for fly strike. I said, 'Lady, you just don't understand. I can show you paddocks out on Warbreccan that are 95,000 acres; you wouldn't see the sheep once in six months. The nearest sheep yards are twenty mile away, and it takes you three days just to get the sheep there.'

She said, 'Well, cut the paddocks up.' So I let her go

on; she had no idea what it was like, and I couldn't tell her.

Flies will kill sheep, given half a chance. Wet areas on the sheep are the worst—around the breech and pizzle and in folds in the skin—in warm wet conditions. In the early 1900s, people began 'jetting' the sheep, spraying them with insecticide. It had become a particular problem because the wrinkly Vermont sheep were becoming infested with blowfly; maybe it had been a problem before then to a certain degree, but the sheep didn't have that much wool on them, and their fleece wasn't as wrinkly.

To jet our sheep, we had a little two-horse-power Lister stationary engine with a high-pressure piston pump and tank. Originally we used to jet with arsenic, but it didn't do man or beast any good. In the 1950s, we starting using the new insecticides—Aldrin was the first to come out, and then Dieldrin and Diazinon. We used to throw the dog into the dip as well if they had fleas or ticks.

To jet them, we had the sheep in a long race; using a handgun or high-pressure hose, we'd spray the insecticide onto the sheep—down their neck and shoulders, and their breech. With the wethers and rams you reached under their bellies, because that was where they'd get blown in a wet season. We probably spent ten seconds on each sheep. (We also used to 'ring' the wethers and rams at crutching—shear a circle around their pizzle as well as their breech, to reduce the chance of fly attack.)

But after we'd been using the insecticides for a few

years, we realised we were getting sick and lethargic all the time—you didn't want to do anything. Alarm bells started to ring. A few people around Longreach were already in hospital, vomiting and lethargic but they didn't immediately connect it to the chemicals as it took months to come on. We only used to jet once a year, but those people had used the insecticides more often. Aldrin, Dieldrin and Diazinon were banned in the 1970s. By then I was getting sick just from the smell of them. They now use safer chemicals for jetting, and graziers have to complete chemical-user certificates to purchase the chemicals so they know how to use them properly, but crutching and mulesing—especially in the merinos—are just as important to keep out the fly. Selective breeding over time put more wool on the sheep, and mulesing came in as a way to minimise fly strike. We usually got a contractor to come in and mules the lambs up to six months of age. The wethers would only get a tiny bit of skin taken off—a strip if they were wrinkly—but the ewes copped a fair bit more. With the ewes, they'd cut out about an inch, or an inch and a half, of skin underneath the vulva and around the breech; if they had a bad wrinkly tail, they'd take all the tail skin off as well, and it grew back as a bare stump. I was against stripping the tail; I thought it was unnecessary. The operation looks terrible, but if you've ever seen thousands of sheep dying from fly strike, like during the shearers' strike in 1956, when the sheep weren't shorn for months in a warm wet year, you can see why it became necessary. You can put this new insecticide oil on now—it softens the mulesed area and speeds up the healing process. After a week, they can run around, no problem, and it's better than them dying.

On one occasion I took my shearing collection to an international shearing competition in Toowoomba. There was a lovely English girl there and she came over to me and asked, 'Mr Tindall, could you tell me about mulesing?' I thought, 'Oh my . . . here we go again,' so I said, 'I'll tell you what—there are four thousand ewes in the yards for the shearing competition. You come with me, if you don't mind hopping over a couple of fences, and I'll show you.'

There was a little pen there with four sheep in it that had been pulled out of the four thousand. Those four sheep hadn't been mulesed; two of them were maggoty, and another had just been flystruck. When they are first struck, there is a tiny little patch on the skin with a little grub in it burrowing down into the sheep, and it then attracts more flies. I said to her, 'Those maggoty ones have been pulled out of a mob of four thousand because they are not mulesed, and there is not one that has been mulesed that has fly strike. Fifty per cent of these non-mulesed sheep are badly struck, and in a fortnight's time both of them will be dead, eaten alive by maggots if they are left untreated.'

There's no problem at all when you can show people why mulesing is so important, they will generally quickly accept that it is necessary, but there are do-gooders who think they know more than people who are growing and caring for the sheep.

Acknowledgements

WRITING IS A solitary pursuit, but I could not have written this book without the help of many.

Thank you firstly to Hugh and Barb Tindall, who welcomed me into their home and lives. It has been an absolute pleasure to work with you and get to know you and your family so well.

My mentor Richard Walsh, whose sage advice I regularly seek; you are a true credit to your profession and a great friend.

The wonderful staff at Regency Park, especially Noo and Chris, thank you for being the computer go-between for Hugh and myself.

Thank you to the wonderful staff at Allen and Unwin, especially my senior editor Siobhán Cantrill; thank you my friend. Once again I had the pleasure of working with Clara Finlay, whose professionalism and common sense is inspiring. Thank you also to Sue Hines and Amy Milne, both dedicated to their profession and delightful women to work with.

Thank you to my long-suffering friends and family, especially Katarina Pearson, Nikki Miller, Annie Green, and the wonderful members of Tuckerbooks Book Club in my hometown of Gundagai, who are a terrific support group, wonderful cooks and put up with my somewhat sporadic attendance.

My family, my backbone—thank you. Hayley, Charlotte and Sam, you always make me happy and I love watching you grow into such caring adults. My darling husband Bert, words are never enough, thank you for your support, your love and your wonderful sense of humour. I love you, mountains even.

Sometimes, especially for a writer, two words don't seem enough, but, thank you.